Dinner of Herbs

An American by birth, Carla Grissmann has spent most of her life outside the United States. She lived for many years in Morocco and has worked in France, Afghanistan, Sri Lanka and Pakistan. She currently lives in London and returns every year to Afghanistan on behalf of the Kabul Museum.
She wrote *Dinner of Herbs* in 1970 when she was forty-two.

Dinner of Herbs

Carla Grissmann

A

ARCADIA BOOKS

LONDON

Arcadia Books Ltd
15–16 Nassau Street
London W1W 7AB

First published in the United Kingdom 2001

A catalogue record for this book is available
from the British Library.

ISBN 1–900850–26–5

Typeset in Stempel Garamond by Discript, London WC2N 4BN
Printed in the United Kingdom by The Cromwell Press, Trowbridge, Wiltshire

Arcadia Books gratefully acknowledges the assistance of Moris Farhi
in checking spellings of the Turkish language in this book.

Arcadia Books distributors are as follows:
in the UK and elsewhere in Europe:
Turnaround Publishers Services
Unit 3, Olympia Trading Estate
Coburg Road
London N22 6TZ

in the USA and Canada:
Consortium Book Sales and Distribution, Inc.
1045 Westgate Drive
St Paul, MN 55114–1065

in Australia:
Tower Books
PO Box 213
Brookvale, NSW 2100

in New Zealand:
Addenda
Box 78224
Grey Lynn
Auckland

in South Africa:
Peter Hyde Associates (Pty) Ltd
PO Box 2856
Cape Town 8000

For Uzak Köy

'Better is a dinner of herbs where love is, than a stalled ox and hatred therewith.'

– Proverbs 15:17

When I left Uzak Köy, I went to New York, to a one-floor clapboard house built in 1825 on now 9th Avenue and 20th Street, that belonged to a friend and that had recently been designated a historical landmark. I was distraught for a long time but in that small house I began to put my thoughts into words – I cannot say put my memories into words because they were not yet memories but part of my daily life. This small volume was the result, written slowly in simple words, as a letter to them, to thank them for having given me so much, for having taught me so much.

Arriving

I had a ticket for the four o'clock bus to Çorak. Earlier that morning I had cautiously eased myself into the turmoil of the new Ankara bus station to try to pick up this final thread of the journey. All the familiar props of the past weeks – Paris, the Orient Express, Istanbul, Ankara – had gradually been stripped away and all I had left now were only two or three meaningless words on a piece of paper.

At the station there seemed to be thousands of people and hundreds of buses reaching into every corner of Turkey. Women with babies on their backs and clusters of solemn, staring children clinging to their skirts stood around the fringes of the crowd, with the old people, to guard the bundles and baskets. The men were forming their own dark clusters around the ticket counters. I went up to a soldier yawning in a heavy crumpled uniform and said to him bluntly, 'Çorak?' as if it were a password he would or would not acknowledge. He smiled and nodded. We pushed past the barkers shouting out the names of cities and towns, and through the uproar around the booths of the various bus companies. Two companies had buses going to Çorak. I was amazed that I had not noticed the big signs ÇORAK the first time around, as the name now seemed to leap out from all the other names. The men behind the ticket counter repeated doubtfully, 'Çorak? Çorak?' several times, as if to confirm that it was really where I wanted to go, not Yozgat or Sıvas or Erzurum, more likely places for foreigners to visit.

When I went back in the afternoon they greeted me with big smiles, and one of the men from behind the counter carried my suitcase out to the platform, got on the bus with me and showed me where to sit. Another world. There were no businessmen here, no women in high-heeled shoes and make-up, no city luggage waiting to be put on top of the bus. There were moustaches and dark unshaven faces, yellow teeth and patched elbows, caps, long dark threadbare overcoats, bundles of brooms, sacks of flour, kerosene lamps tied in bunches. The suitcases were round wicker baskets with a piece of cloth neatly tucked in over the top and sewn down all around the rim with soft white string, or old blankets tied with rope, easy to swing over your shoulder, easy to lift up and pack down on top of the bus between the other sacks and crates and baskets.

Çorak lies 250 kilometres from Ankara, off the main highway that cuts through the centre of Turkey from east to west, across the vast Anatolian plateau of Asia Minor stretching from Istanbul to the Persian frontier. Our bus was going directly to Çorak and no further. Many of the men were talking in groups and seemed to know each other. Not many women travel on buses, and at the ticket window they had protectively seated all the women together two by two, even separating them from their husbands if they needed an extra woman to fill the second seat. I sat next to a beaming old lady wearing baggy bloomers down to her ankles, wide skirts over them and an orange nylon sweater inside out. A frayed headscarf was wound across her chin and covered most of her face. She gave me some walnuts and a little apple dug out of her skirts.

Half-way to Çorak the bus stopped at one of the many *lokanta*, restaurants, along the highway. Some are bright and modern, but most of them are bare, a faded blue or turquoise, filled with cigarette smoke and the smell of cooking. Other buses were parked at odd angles outside, their passengers spread out at the tables. A new group arrived, a group left. You went up to the open counter or directly into the kitchen and pointed out what you wanted from the dozen huge black pots on the wood-burning stove, and the plates were brought to your table at a run. The toilets were outside, in rough cement blocks with wooden doors and wet floors and rusty tin cans on the floor under a faucet, for the water that is used instead of paper.

I sat at a table with a young man and his younger wife with her scarf between her teeth and a baby on her lap. For some reason he spoke French, and swayed back and forth on his chair in his relish to speak. Before he said anything he limbered up by hissing through his teeth to himself at high speed: '*Je suis tu es il est nous sommes vous êtes!*' Then he launched out, '*Allemande! Vous êtes allemande?*'

Another rapid whistling: '*Je vais tu vas il va nous allons vous allez!*' and then to me, '*Où vous allez?*'

In French I told him I was going to Çorak, and then on to a village called Uzak Köy and that tomorrow I hoped I was meeting a friend called Kâmuran, who was the teacher in the village where I was going. He listened ecstatically, all the while rubbing his hands on his knees and rocking back and forth on his seat. Again he went down the line hissing through his teeth and said, '*La Turquie, la Turquie, vous aimez?*'

'Do you like Turkey, do you love Turkey?' that was always the ringing question.

'Yes, yes, I love Turkey, it is beautiful, the people are so kind, they are good people.'

'But we are poor.'

'Maybe you are poor, in one way. But you have a beautiful country, you have beautiful children, and big hearts...'

Nodding and smiling, they always agree.

When we got back on the bus all the men who had seemed to look right through me, stopped him, pulled on his arm and asked him where I was going. I had told him that I was American, but that had not meant much to him and he explained to the others that I was French and was going to teach at a school in Uzak Köy. A young man directly in front of me bolted around and said he knew this village. We discovered he also knew Kâmuran, as they were both teachers, and he said, 'Don't worry about anything. We will find Kâmuran, maybe even tonight.'

I looked out the window, half in wonder, half acutely

aware of where I was, so strangely at ease in this unfamiliar world. It was extraordinary to be here after all, to be sitting in this bus on this day.

Late last spring I had spent two months in Ürgüp, one of the larger villages of Cappadocia, in central Anatolia. I was one morning sitting benevolently on a stone wall in the sun near the post office. Two young men came down the street toward me.

'Do you speak English?' one of them said rather roughly.

I had heard this so often that I answered back also rather roughly, 'No!' and they walked on.

That evening I went to have supper at a small place called the *Kulüp* and I was reading on the flat roof upstairs where some tables were set up at random. The young man who had spoken to me was there and he came over. He did not look Turkish. His hair was light and thin, his eyes a silver green and his face smooth and calm. He was not smiling.

'I am sorry. You were angry. I did not mean to make you angry. We saw you sitting, we thought you are a boy. My friend said, Let us go and talk. That is all.'

He spoke in slow words and I knew I had made a mistake.

'Please sit down. I was the one who was rude. What is your name?' I asked him.

'Kâmuran.'

'Kâmuran anything else?'

'Yes, Çayir.

'Çayir . . . does your name mean something?'

'*Çayir* means field, a green field. We have many names like that. Simple names, names of things. What is your name?'

I told him my name was Carla, but that it did not mean anything. He smiled for the first time.

'Yes, in Turkish it means a veil. There are many veils, *carlar her tarafta*, you see?'

'What a nice way to learn Turkish, with people's names. Do you work, Kâmuran? What is your work?'

'I am teacher, I am teacher in a village. Ürgüp is my own village, and I am now here in my own house in the summer. The village of my school is far from here.'

We ate together, and we talked. He searched for his English, speaking very slowly, yet I understood everything he wanted to say. He talked about the village where he taught and the school, about his discouragement, his ambition, and in my mind I was trying to visualize what his life was. I tried to make a picture with the faltering words village, forty houses, 300 people in all, no electricity, no road, walking from one village to another with his hands full of stones to throw at the dogs that leapt around him.

Through those late spring weeks we were often together, with his friends. In the evenings they all met at Veli's handicraft shop on the little main street. Veli and Kâmuran had grown up side by side and they were like brothers together. Veli spoke English recklessly.

'What work does your father do?' I asked him once when he had talked about his father.

'He is a watermelon.'

'Veli!'

'I mean, he is ... shoemaker. Not watermelon. Your long English words are all the same for me,' he laughed.

Veli had a small room in the back of the shop, with reed matting on the walls, a low bench and cushions along three sides and two big metal trays in the centre as tables. A door opened onto the back alley. Whoever was sitting nearest the door, without getting up, would lean over and open it a crack, lean out into the street until someone trotted into sight and then give out orders for cheese and bread, olives, cigarettes, raki, or whatever was needed at the time. Minutes later things would begin arriving, from the restaurant at the end of the alley or the shop next door or the market, and be briskly passed from the dark alley into the room.

There was always music. Veli sang and played the *saz*, the eight-string Turkish guitar. He had learned without lessons, the gift was innate. Lying back on the cushions I watched the blurred mosaic pattern of colour spreading over the darkened ceiling from an old lantern of cut glass. The slender metallic music filled the room.

'What was that song about?'

'It was about love.'

As Veli played, one of the men sat upright against the wall, his hands on his knees, his eyes staring ahead. He raised his head, began to sing, in long filigreed phrases, his body moving with the movement of his voice.

'That was also a song about love,' said Veli.

The room was full of smoke and men in dark shabby jackets, open shirts and heavy mud-caked shoes. The *saz* was passed to one of the older men, who strummed a soft, slow melody. Several voices followed the song. Someone leaned over and said, 'Do you know what this song is? What means *ninni*? It is the sweet words for the baby when it sleeps.'

I looked around the room and thought in disbelief, 'These men are singing a lullaby.'

They took me to the local theatre, a dusty room in the attic of an old wooden house, with everyone there like a big picnic. There were several short plays, all with the same young actors, stuffed with pillows or tottering on a cane with flour on their hair. They waved and chatted into the audience. One little boy sitting next to us was laughing so hard he kept falling out of his chair. Kâmuran translated punch-lines when he could: 'Your donkey is dead, too!' and, 'Well, your brass pot just had a baby pot in *my* house,' with everyone shrieking with laughter. Kâmuran was laughing so much himself each time he set the little boy back onto his chair that he had tears running down his face, and I did too in the end.

We went many places around Ürgüp, on bicycles and once on a motorcycle which belonged to the man who made all the false teeth in Ürgüp. We climbed into the old cave churches and sat and looked over the small narrow valleys and always Kâmuran's village was at the centre of our talk.

For a long time I had wanted to touch the life of a Turkish village, knowing how remote it was from the classical splendours of Istanbul or the Ionian coast, and how different it must be from a Muslim village in North Africa, but I knew I could not approach a village alone. As Kâmuran talked that spring, as I made him talk and describe his life, the village where he taught began to take on a new reality. No foreigner had ever been there, but they were open and kind people, he said. I told him I wanted to see his village.

'You would not like it...' he said briefly.

Later he said, 'Read *Bizim Köy* or *Mehmet, My Hawk*. They are books about villages, it will tell you about our village people. You do not know what it is like. People starve, they have only old newspapers to cover new babies with to keep warm, the dogs eat what you put out of your body. People kill each other, they die with hate...'

We talked often of where wisdom came from, of where love came from. How fragile it all must be at one point, the planting and growing of life, a man's life or that of a village, in one direction or another.

'My village is like the others, but it is lucky I think. There is much love between the people there. There is another village near mine, I do not like it – the people have made themselves ugly, they have narrow eyes when they look up and I always walk through without stopping. It is like walking through a dangerous place.'

Kâmuran, I think for the first time, began to put into words, perhaps into conscious thought, the things that surrounded him. I continued to ask him, why could I not go to his village? He in the beginning would have to be the link between them and myself and later I could perhaps bring forward a part of the outside world that he was trying to open their minds to. Why was it not possible?

'They love with village love,' he said later, 'and someone like you, you know only city love. You would not understand.'

'Maybe you could live in the Muhtar's house,' he said a few days later.

On the last night that late spring we all got drunk on music and raki in the back of Veli's shop. At four in the morning in front of my pale blue hotel we all shook hands and said goodbye, and again the next morning at the bus station.

'About my village, you must think,' Kâmuran said nervously, standing by the bus door, 'you do not know what it is like.'

That summer I wrote several businesslike letters from France with numbered questions. Kâmuran went back to the village to talk to the Muhtar and the Elders. He asked them if they would allow a foreigner, a stranger, a woman, to be a guest in their village for a while. They had all said yes, of course, yes. Kâmuran sent me a businesslike letter in return. He drew a crooked map of how to get there. He printed ANKARA in big stiff letters, then Çorak smaller, and a smaller Bulutlu, and then Uzak Köy very small at the end of the road, almost off the bottom of the page.

*

The bus was now nearing Çorak. People were beginning to sit up.

'Are there hotels in Çorak?' I asked the man in front of me.

'Oh yes, but only one for you, nice and clean and not much money.'

It was pitch dark by then. As the small lights of Çorak appeared to the right, some of the men around me began pointing and smiling and turning around to say, 'PAHris ... PAHris ...' We pulled up on the small main street, two blocks long beginning near the rail tracks and ending in a wide unpaved square scattered with jeeps and carts and minibuses parked for the night. We got out on a muddy street with narrow broken pavements. A tractor lurched by, a donkey, some unsteady old men in long dark coats; a few boys in tattered clothes hovered around the bus door. Two or three shops were still open, with men in shirt-sleeves leaning on the counters reading newspapers and smoking, and on each street corner a dimly-lit tea-house packed with sombre figures playing cards at small crude tables, indistinct in the grey smoke of their endless cigarettes. Several young boys grabbed my suitcase, and the teacher and two other men came along to show me the hotel.

We squeezed through a narrow glass door into a room where some men were sitting in a row, in white shirts, caps and dark jackets, smoking and listening to a small transistor radio on the desk. There was only one room left, with two beds. It was 5 lira a bed, about 20 pence, but since I was alone I had to take both beds. The teacher and two men from the hotel and the little boys with my suitcase climbed up the narrow stairs. When I left France a friend had given me a set of wheels on a long metal pole that you strap to a suitcase. It had all come apart, I was carrying it and the teacher asked appreciatively if it was a movie camera.

The room had translucent glass double doors and

one wall was also glass doors, leading into the adjoining room. There were two iron bedsteads, one chair, a table in the corner, a limp sallow towel hanging on a nail, under each bed a pair of wooden clogs. The single light bulb dangling from the ceiling stroked vague shadows on the grey walls. The teacher made gestures about locking myself in and putting the key under the pillow. He was going out to look for Kâmuran and said he would come back shortly.

There were steps and voices and suddenly the light went on in the next room. Through the milky glass doors I could see two dark blurred figures moving around and could hear them talking and the creaking of the bedsprings as they sat down. I could see the hunched back of one of the men as he tried to get comfortable on his bed. The teacher came back a few minutes later and said that Kâmuran was not in Çorak. I wondered how he had hoped to find him anyway in a town of 12,000 people, but I know now there were only two small streets where he could be, and even simpler than that, you could stop anyone on the street and ask if he were there and they would know.

'Tomorrow morning I come back, we look for him then. Do you need anything now? Tea? Something to eat?'

No, there was nothing, and we said good-night. Five minutes later a little boy appeared with a tiny glass of tea, a miniature tin spoon, and two lumps of sugar wetly melting in the saucer. I pulled the string of the light, lay down on the bed and tried to sleep, tried to blend my sleep into this bed, this room, this street.

There are many reasons why people are where they are and go where they are going. An evasion, a search, a return, a need to see for oneself, a path continued. I was here now. Were the sheets clean? They seemed clean. Did it matter though? Was the towel clean? It had been washed threadbare and hung to dry in a damp courtyard. Did it matter that the faded red curtains were sagging unevenly, torn off their rings at both ends, or that I had washed in a cracked stone sink out of a bucket of cold water in a windowless room with a rough slimy floor? That I had seen only the sombre colours of shabby clothing, and unfamiliar faces? That I did not really understand their words, their course of life, did not really know where I was going, had never been here before? No, none of this mattered, these were not the important things. Not when you are held in that secret joy, that serenity which comes when you know without knowing, beyond even thought, that you are where you want to be, that you are listening to the music your inner ear is straining to hear, that you are, too, like the nomad who for one night has found shelter and can sleep in peace.

I woke up at six. All the rooms were already empty, the doors standing open. It was a beautiful day and I stood on the little balcony, ate the bananas and dried cake I had brought from Ankara, and watched the early morning street below. I had written Kâmuran saying I would be in Çorak on Friday morning, 18 September, which was today, and I was now wondering rather anxiously what shape the day would take.

There was a loud knocking on the door. It was the

teacher from the night before, breathing heavily and very pleased.

'Come, come. Kâmuran is here.'

We went downstairs and outside, just as Kâmuran was coming round the corner. I had not seen him since that late spring, yet it seemed quite natural to be shaking hands again at seven in the morning on the corner of this little town in Anatolia. He seemed older somehow, his hair thinner, his face more drawn, but his steady gaze had not changed.

'Welcome,' he said uneasily.

The tea-houses were setting out a few rickety chairs and tables on the street. We sat down, ordered tea and had our shoes shined by a little boy with a wooden box strapped on his back, ready for the day's work. Kâmuran looked depressed, and I had a fleeting horrible thought that what had all seemed so natural perhaps wasn't natural at all. Was all this too much responsibility for him, as well as for me? Kâmuran sent a boy for some soup and bread. He shivered, he had been up since three that morning, had walked eight kilometres in the dark to Bulutlu to get the old farm bus to Çorak, the same bus we were shortly going to take back.

'Kâmuran, please don't worry. I've lived in many places, fancy places and simple places, and the simple places are always the best. Electricity, all those things, hot water, telephones, big shops, not important.'

'Yes, you say, but you do not know. You can say because you always have a choice. This is different, there is no choice, this is the way it is.'

The boy came back with the soup. It was made

from bones, boiled with garlic, sensationally giving off its smell. It was delicious. Kâmuran cheered up manifestly, and so did I. Some boys carried my things to the square and helped lift them on top of the bus that was beginning to fill up for its return trip to Bulutlu. It was an ancient, squat Ford bus, painted bright blue, with many layers of dented and chipped paint, skeletal metal seats and ragged holes in the metal floor. Kâmuran put me on the bench in front and went to buy cigarettes, carrots and newspapers.

'Do you have a torch?' he asked me.

'Torch?'

'You sit. I buy.'

He looked depressed again, although he laughed. 'You see? You do *not* know what is a village.'

An incredible number of smiling people were packing into the bus, sitting in the aisle on bags of grain and flour. Six of us were wedged onto the bench under the windscreen, with a little boy actually fitted in at the last moment on the driver's left side, under his arm.

We went uphill most of the time, creeping and groaning along the dirt road, climbing through deserted country, over ridge after ridge of barren, treeless hills. The wheat had just been cut and the slopes were shorn dry, there was not a soul in sight for miles and miles, then suddenly a slim dark figure, going where? coming from where? on this endless horizon of hills receding further and further into the haze of the sun. We passed through several villages where the dogs leapt out and savagely chased the tyres of the bus out past the last house. The bus stopped from time to time, a few people climbing down and with their bundles over their shoulders set out across the empty, straw-coloured landscape although there was not a house or a village to be seen. Everyone knew each other, laughing and talking from one end of the bus to the other. Two hours later we got to Bulutlu, a village too, but with a one-room mud post office, a one-room mud tea-house, a gendarme outpost and a new agricultural bank painted bright pink. By luck there was a jeep stopped there and Kâmuran bargained with the driver to take us to Uzak Köy.

The road branched off to the left, more a rutted track than a road, and several times the driver had almost to stop the jeep as it swayed and pitched over the rocky shelf of a stream and across the deep troughs of hardened mud. We drove through two small villages, the colourless flat-roofed houses low against the colourless earth, and each time Kâmuran said, 'No, not yet, but it is the same.' If you squinted your eyes the thirty or forty small mud houses clustered together on the slope seemed to dematerialize, to blend back into their original earth. If it were not for the bright clothing of the women, like drops of pure enamel on a tawny canvas, and the running children and the breath of smoke from the chimney stumps, you could think you were looking at an uninhabited landscape, the unbroken expanse only here and there imperceptibly troubled, as if a giant finger had reached down and idly stirred the smooth surface into little random eddies of earth-shaped houses.

Then there was no longer any road at all, only a

faint trail around and across the tops of the hills. We came into Uzak Köy suddenly, driving over a rise and down a long narrow path between scattered houses, and pulled up in front of the Muhtar's house in an open area more or less in the centre of the village.

Uzak Köy was held in the cupped palm of a rise of high land, overlooking a broad dry river bed crawling out of sight around the feet of the retreating hills. Low in the distance a long line of mountains stretched across the far horizon. The forty-odd houses that sheltered the inhabitants of the village all faced in the same direction, open to the sun. They seemed identical, the new ones different only in their newness. At the bottom of the village, a small area of land that caught the overflow of water from the spring was marked off by low mud and stone walls into long rectangular strips of gardens. The only trees, you could count these graceful shimmering poplars on one hand, grew along this same invisible path of precious water.

A swarm of children appeared on all sides. Some women with babies on their backs came towards us. In the background some men stood watching, dark and aloof. There were smiling women on the whitewashed stoop in front of the door and they reached down and pulled my suitcase up the three bumpy steps formed from flat uneven boulders. We took our shoes off and went into the main room of the Muhtar's house, the central meeting place for everyone of the village. The room was broad and cheerful, the raised mud floor covered with mats, with larger flat cushions placed squarely along three walls and fat bolsters propped along the sides. A shiny kerosene lamp swung from a beam of the low ceiling. A white cat was sleeping on a little pillow in a window niche in the sun and there was a piece of newspaper tacked across one broken pane.

Kâmuran and I, as guests, were put in the two corners, where you can drape both arms over the back of the bolsters on either side and sit with your legs stretched out in front of you. Hacı İsmail, the Muhtar, was at a wedding in another village, so there were only his mother, his wife, two sons, two daughters-in-law and other family members around us. The door opened and closed and more women came in, beaming and staring, with many children pushing past them, giggling and scuffling. They were scolded away like a flock of birds and another batch blew in as soon as the door opened again. Two men appeared at the door. In an instant the women had risen and slid out of the room. Only the women of the house were left. The men were smiling, 'Welcome, welcome,' they said. Others came in. They knew someone from another country was coming to visit their village; they wanted to see what this meant and to ask questions.

'You are rich. Why do you want to live with poor people?'

'What is there to see here? We have nothing!'

'Why do you want to come here, when we want to go somewhere else?'

Kâmuran translated quietly back and forth and they nodded their heads. The questions they asked were questions that should have been asked, that I had hoped they would ask, as it made me feel, because I understood their questions, that their reality was not so different from my reality, and that I could answer them with a truth that would be their truth. That first hour we had also roared with laughter at the same thing at the same moment – a little boy had come gleefully bouncing into the room and, when he caught sight of me, had stopped dead in his tracks, his expression changing into one of such utter horror that we all burst out laughing and the little boy burst into tears.

There were other questions, which made me see in what way they tried to place me in their own conception of life.

'Does your father have sheep?' they asked.

'No . . .' I was speechless.

'Does he have land?'

'No.'

'Does your mother work?' and one of the men made the gesture of digging in the soil.

'No.'

'In your country, do you eat *pekmez* and boiled wheat?' When I said no again, they shook their heads and slapped one upturned hand into the other and said, '*Vah, vah, vah,*' in compassion and pity.

The Muhtar's son brought in a big tin tray and set it in the centre of the floor, laid out wooden spoons and stacks of limp folded bread, and then carried in a white enamel dish with two eggs scrambled in oil and a big bowl of boiled wheat. Kâmuran and I and several of the men hitched up around the tray. Hacı Kadin, the Muhtar's mother, sat back against the wall with the other men. It was her right as she was older, and also venerated in the region for her kindness and wisdom, and the fact that she had been to Mecca. She was short and square, with a head like a Roman emperor. Most of her teeth were gone and the lines of her face were cut deep from smiling. She had on what looked like a man's dark-blue pin-striped suit jacket from the 1920s, men's grey socks and a wide skirt over baggy bloomers. A white scarf wound around her head and chin, held with another scarf tied Red-Indian fashion across her forehead. Later she took my hand and looked at my long nails, shook her head, laughed, and patted my arm.

They talked about a place for me to live, a room in one of the houses. Hacı Kadin said I could sleep with her, but I tried to explain that that would be difficult because I read at night and sometimes typed letters, and it was better if I could have a room alone. There was an empty house in the village, but they all said it would not be right for me to be alone in an empty house. There was a family, a good family and very poor, where the husband was away working in İzmir. They had a room. It seemed to have been decided then, without consulting the family concerned, and at mid-afternoon, with several little boys energetically carrying my suitcase, and one carrying the set of wheels, we went up the slope to see the room. The house was like all the others, one floor of mud and straw on a base of stone, a small central room with a dug-out hollow in the wall at the far end for the fire, for cooking, for heat, and a larger room off each side.

Asiye Nedihe, the head of the household while her son was away, came out on the stoop in her socks, drying her hands on her skirts, wheezing and flustered and smiling. I could hardly believe my eyes when I saw her. A white scarf was wound around her old head, the ends tied in a knot on the top of her head like two tiny rabbit ears. Wisps of bright orange hennaed hair poked out around her toothless face. She was small and slightly hunched, I felt enormous next to her. When she walked, she scuttled. She took snuff; much later I brought her some from Dunhill's in New York, By Appointment to His Late Majesty George V, but she locked it in the wooden chest with all her other possessions. She too wore an old pin-striped suit jacket and whenever I patted her shoulder small clouds of dust flew up. She wore men's socks and her two dusty dry big toes stuck out of holes in the front, and the heels were gone. She cried easily, and often, as she had terrible memories of her sons, her bright eyes streaming as she sat on the floor, rocking back and forth, weeping and blowing her nose in her skirts. She was the fairy-tale grandmother, whose flurries of indignation or anger were greeted with teasing arms of love wound around her stooped shoulders, who laughed like a child with the children, who kept all the people of her family strongly growing around her old roots. But of course I saw only a small part of this that first day.

The room I was to live in was quite large, with two windows on one side and one at the end wall. The floor was packed mud and straw and so were the walls, although they had been whitewashed once or twice a long time ago. The ceiling was laid with smooth long poplar beams about a foot apart, supporting the latticed reed matting which held the packed mud roof. There was a huge fancy aluminium bed, one of two in the village, a big wooden box on its side with a broken glass pane; a built-up mud ledge along the wall under the windows had flat square cushions for sitting and straw bolsters for your back. In another corner a small area of floor had been roughly spread with cement: the bathroom. A small hole went outside through which to empty your washing water. At various heights along the walls there were big nails to hang things on. A large pastel-tinted photograph of Asiye Nedihe's son tilted out way over your head; you had to stand almost directly under it and look up to get any sort of proper perspective of his face. No table, no chair, no lock on the crude wooden door. I could already see where I would put my books and, by pulling the box against the side of the bed, make a nest for reading at night, the few insignificant things that suddenly make a room one's own.

They left me there and I stood in the middle of the floor without moving, suspended. In the next room there was much noise of voices and people pushing against the door. I opened my suitcase and began taking things out. The door burst open and a crowd of women and children surged in. Most of them had never been outside of their village and had never seen a foreigner, yet they all seemed delighted to see me, touching my hair and fingernails and picking up each thing I had unpacked. Everything seemed to strike them as funny, and the older women kept patting me as they laughed. I could hear the sound of their calloused hands catching on my nylon bathrobe as they passed it around, like toast being rubbed together. Asiye Nedihe tried to keep order, pouncing on the children and wedging them out the door. She said she would sleep on the floor by my bed at night if I were afraid. After they had all left, the air circulated with dust, the floor was littered with walnut shells and potato peels, from the small warm potatoes they kept pulling out of their skirts and offering around. One tiny black rubber baby shoe lay near the door.

It was already dark when Kâmuran came to take me to his little room in the schoolhouse, not far away. His kerosene stove was broken, so he had set out only olives, bread and honey, and we sat on the floor and had our supper. He looked at me sideways, warily.

'Is everything all right?'

'Well, look at me,' I said. 'Can't you tell? You must teach me the words in Turkish for joy ... for gratitude...'

He walked home with me that first night, weaving the flashlight through the darkness and kicking off the neighbour's dog who had rushed up fiercely. It was not yet eight o'clock but the front door of my house was closed and there was only a faint light inside. I pounded on the door and felt bad that I had to wake them up, although by now several other dogs had arrived in a frenzy and were barking thunderously in a semicircle in front of the house. Elif, Asiye Nedihe's daughter-in-law, who had brought the aluminium bed as part of her dowry, opened the door, shouted at the dogs and they vanished in the dark.

The floor of the small centre room was almost entirely covered with bedding, indistinct mounds of sleeping forms burrowed under the heavy wool covers, not a face or head visible. Seven people fitted together in sleep on the mud floor. We stepped over them and into my room. Elif had pulled closed the little cotton curtains, stacked the big pillows from the bed onto the mud ledge. She lit the kerosene lamp on the wooden box and showed me a bucket of water near the little hole in the floor, and with a big smile said good-night.

With difficulty I worked out how I would brush my teeth and wash down the hole, using the water sparingly. I got into bed on the lumpy wool mattress, wondering about how I would get up. I found out soon enough that the day started at 5.30. There was an unbelievable clatter and talking outside my door. I put the pillow over my head and twice a crowd came in and I could sense a group of people standing around my bed having a good look and talking in hushed voices. I got up at 6.30 and managed to get dressed in between visits.

Those First Days

The first days were without form. I began slowly to dare to go out on my own, down to the spring to fill my bucket with water, into the houses that pulled me inside, learning the names of the children, learning how to refuse or accept tea or food. There were non-stop meals, at all times, improvised it seemed, with other people's children and anyone who happened to be there solidly eating away. There were potatoes, bulgur wheat, and white beans and once or twice a slice of white cold sugar beet, which seemed the most delicious thing in the world. Sometimes there were eggs, one or two, floating in a bowl of oil, two eggs for six people, but they got more and more scarce with the cold weather, and soon there was no milk or yoghurt or anything fresh or green. A man and a horse came by, a phantasmagoric apparition over the crest of the hill, selling apples. He weighed them out, holding the scales up high, with a big rock on one side and the apples on the other. We ate walnuts and *pekmez*, the thick brown grape syrup, and always bread, piled up like big thin pancakes, that you wrapped around a slice of raw onion or tore into smaller pieces and fashioned into little scoops, for soup.

*

Quickly the days became a pattern, and things that had bewildered or amused or astounded me became natural and simple. Kâmuran's patience never faltered. I began to understand the questions they asked him about me, and his answers, and could soon answer them myself. My father's name, that he had no land, no sheep, that I didn't have any brothers or sisters, that we had dogs and spoons in my country too, that I wasn't married because in my country we can accept or refuse as we wish and women can be alone and independent and happy that way, and that I might get married later, when I was, say, sixty. This thought caused only expressions of horror.

The hardest thing for me to get accustomed to was the total lack of privacy. At night each family bolted the front door of their house, but during the day the doors were always open. There was no lock on the door to my room and people came in at any time. From the beginning I tried very hard to ask them to knock first, as it was a shock when suddenly the door burst open and a group of people came in. The neighbours and regular visitors did learn to knock in a way, but the results were the same, if not worse. They hit the door, with a shattering blow with the flat of their hand, and *then* burst into the room, so I jumped twice each time.

The women took great pleasure in visiting each other's houses and sitting around talking. It was part of the structure of their day and on the innumerable times I visited a house I never once sensed that it was importune or that I was intruding. Quite the opposite: every visit had the quality of a special occasion, as if I had come from a long way away. This was not reserved only for me; whenever anyone at all entered there was always a welcoming cry and room made on the floor, a cushion patted and hands reaching up to pull the person down amongst them. Sometimes I left my house in the early morning, with my bucket to get water, and I would not get home until supper time. I would be carried all over the village from house to house on an irresistible wave of activity, eating steadily all the way. There always seemed so much to talk about.

During the mornings I most often sat in my room on my mud window ledge, to read or study Turkish or type letters. When any men came to visit they never knocked, and I felt it would have been presumptuous to ask them to. They simply came in, kicking off their shoes, and went directly over to the mud ledge, sat down and pulled their feet up under them. I passed out cigarettes and little tin ashtrays and asked if they would like tea. Any women who happened to be in the room would vanish without a word. It was different when one of the younger men came to the house. The women remained where they were, talking and joking with him, and he would sit among them. Whenever Dursun, a boisterous and good-natured young man, arrived he would plant his cap on Asiye Nedihe's old head, pick her off her feet and swing her around and set her down, indignant and giggling like a girl. Dursun would sit for hours in front of the fire, laughing and chatting and eating whatever they gave him.

In theory there was supposed to be a mail delivery

to the village once a week, but it never happened that way. On one trip through Bulutlu a man came running out of the tea-house with some letters for me that had been there for weeks. Another time, we went to see the teacher in the next village and just before leaving he casually took down two letters for me from a little shelf where the teapots were kept. Once in the middle of a card-playing evening one of the men I didn't know very well reached into his breast pocket and without a word pulled out a letter for me, all warm and wrinkled. Sometimes a group of children, mute with importance, brought a letter at the crack of dawn, right up to my bed. Most of these letters had been opened in a friendly way, which I didn't mind at all. In one fashion or another, everything seemed to arrive, although I never divined any discernible postal system at work or the hand of an actual postman anywhere in the background.

There were no tables or chairs. I had put one of the large flat pillows on my suitcase and I typed on that, sitting cross-legged on the ledge, with a straw bolster to lean against. The women who came to visit never really understood what I meant when I dared to ask them to come back later because I wanted to 'work'. They patted me and said, 'Good, good . . . you work,' as they climbed up and settled around me up and down the ledge. It didn't bother them if I read or typed, so how could they bother me if they just sat around amiably visiting. When I stopped and got out the cigarettes, they said, 'No, no . . . you work . . . work.' Sometimes there were as many as ten women with their babies and smaller children between their knees, banked up all around. At a baby's slightest whimper they reached down into their dresses and pulled out a heavy white breast and set the baby onto it. Even after it had fallen asleep and had sunk down into their skirts they continued chatting and cracking walnuts and smoking, with their breast out. One morning, Meryem, from next door, was sitting on one fat haunch on the ledge right up against me. She had been nursing her baby, Nepuria, and Nepuria had finished and was playing with her mother's breast. She had it in both her tiny fists and suddenly a fine spurt of milk squirted in a thin arc directly on to my typewriter and the page I was writing. Meryem snatched her breast away and looked at me anxiously, but it was very funny and everyone roared with laughter.

There was nothing they loved more than this sort of thing, that could be recounted later with amplified gestures and dialogue. The most trivial incident took on the dimensions of a story. One afternoon there was a quarrel on the other side of the village, between Suna and Kezban, two young women whose houses adjoined. We could hear the shouting quite clearly and we went out on the stoop to watch the two small figures shaking their fists and coming and going around each other. It was not serious, some trouble over Kezban's dog, but this sort of thing was rare and because of that it drew a scattered audience from almost every house. Very early the next morning Kezban was over on our side of the village, going through the whole story again in a loud voice to Meryem. Somehow they disagreed and began a small fight of their own. I could hear them shouting at each other from my bed. Later I saw Meryem and, wanting to tease her a little bit, I said, 'Meryem, I was sleeping so nicely in my bed this morning when suddenly, suddenly, I heard two big chickens begin to squawk and flap their wings at each other, such a noise ... did you hear them, these chickens?' I couldn't say all this word for word in good Turkish of course, but with the words I knew and a lot of easy pantomime and chicken squawks I made myself understood, hoping at the same time I was not going too far. Meryem listened, frowning, and slowly her face broke into an ecstatic smile and she began slapping her thigh and doubling over with laughter. For days people came up to me and said eagerly, 'What is the story of the big chickens in front of your window?' Even Kezban herself came over, wanting to hear it and wiping her eyes from laughter.

When you are learning a new language I think you inevitably use a great deal of pantomime and mimicry, and develop small speech idiosyncracies, much of which is naturally expressed through the comic. Beyond the clownish aspect of this can lie true humour, and if you can genuinely share this most subtle and personal sensibility, I think you have won half the battle of human communication. Although the people in the village were extremely reserved in their speech and their manners, and did not seem to express themselves with gesture or emotion, they were an enthusiastic audience and instantly caught the slightest flicker of whimsy and the illusive point of any story. We built up between us a special language and a mutual way of teasing that never ceased to move me, even after endless repetition. Their teasing of each other and of me was a warm human thing and seemed to me to be a part of wisdom, an open, guileless generosity of heart. It takes a certain bigness in people to know that you only tease the person you love and respect.

Everyone in the village loved Salih. He was one of the poorest men, had many children and debts and went off periodically to Ankara to look for work. While he was gone they missed him and wondered how he was. In the evenings in Hacı İsmail's house when they played records on the little battery-run turntable, Salih would get up and dance, one hand behind his back, slowly gyrating and stomping in the centre of the smoke-clouded room, and everyone clapped their hands to the music and in applause. He had an enormous appetite and his stomach was one of the things he was always teased about. I had bought several giant wooden soup ladles in Ankara for friends in America, and one evening during Ramazan I put one of them in my skirt to take along to the evening meal we had all been invited to. Salih was always one of the guests, and just before we began to eat I presented him with the ladle, again hoping it would not be misunderstood. Salih seized the ladle, instantly removed the regular spoon from his place and chuckled with pleasure, all the men around him thumping him on the back and laughing. He couldn't actually use it, it was too big, but every night thereafter he arrived at the various houses with the ladle under his arm and laid it solemnly in front of him on the tray.

People in the Village

I had been there about ten days when a group of women came to visit. Most of them took their shoes off outside the door and the rest kicked them off inside the room, before stepping up on the slightly raised mud floor. They went around the room examining everything in sight, and then came over to the ledge and settled down all around me, legs helter-skelter, forming a solid frieze of dusty feet, chapped, cracked hands, brightly coloured bloomers, skirts, sweaters, scarves, babies and smiling faces. I had been wearing all these days a pair of brown wool trousers and a man's turtleneck sweater, and when I went out a black knitted cap over my hair. Nobody had made any comment, but this morning, one of the older women hitched up closer and with her hand on my knee, she said:

'You know, what you are wearing, it's very ugly. Why don't you wear what we wear? *This* is pretty . . . *şu da güzel*,' pinching up a fold of her blue and orange bloomers, 'and *this* is pretty,' pointing to someone's skirt with pink and yellow orchids outlined in black swirling across it. 'But your dress, not pretty, very ugly.'

She was quite right, of course, and I instantly saw

how awful I must look to them, in straight pants and no skirts, almost indecent actually, and definitely without taste. They had brought Donush with them, who did all the sewing in the village on an old pedal sewing machine that had been part of her dowry. The machine was installed in the sitting-room of her house, a good two feet off the ground at one end of the room on its own mud ledge. She charged 2 lira to make a pair of bloomers and 3 lira to make a skirt. The next time I went to Çorak I brought back three yards of wild purple and green and red apples for the bloomers, and for the skirt three yards of yellow and orange lightning streaks going in all directions on a black background. The women liked these materials very much. '*Bak, ne güzel,*' they said, 'Look how pretty.'

Donush measured for the bloomers with a long piece of string, from the waist to below the knees, and tied a knot in the string, and the same thing for the skirt only a little shorter knots in the string. She folded the material according to the knots and then folded it again and sliced through the cloth with a heavy knife. The two large pieces were for the legs, and a much smaller piece which had miraculously appeared was fitted in the crotch so you could sit easily cross-legged with your knees wide apart. When she had all the pieces sewed together it looked like an enormous flat bag, but with the string in the waist and in the two cuffs, it ballooned into a neat pair of bloomers.

Only a few houses had any sort of mirror, and these were hung high up on the walls, slanting out at a 35-degree angle, so your head loomed largely and your feet were barely visible. The mirror in Donush's house had been shattered years ago by a festive bullet fired off during a wedding celebration, but the women stood under it nevertheless, squinting up cheerfully at their splintered kaleidoscopic reflections.

The left-over scraps of material were immediately snatched away. The women patched even the smallest pieces together to make covers for their babies, or a pocket for a skirt, or a pot-holder or napkin to wrap the hot bread in. Meryem sewed together a tiny old lady's dress for her baby out of a left-over strip of curtain material from Kâmuran's one window. Elif had just made a little patchwork quilt and I found in one corner a small triangle of my lightning streaks. 'Ha! Mine!' I laughed, and we began going over the whole quilt, picking out the various patches and naming the original owner. By this time I knew the women and their clothes well enough and was just as good as Elif at putting a name to each patch.

In the village there was one store, a windowless little mud room with rough plank shelves on one wall. It was more or less Hacı İsmail's shop, that is, he had the key to the big padlock on the door and if you wanted something you had to find him first. He stocked sugar, cigarettes, candles, socks, salt, thread and needles, kerosene and wicks for the lamps, matches, rubber shoes, and a few other things lying dustily around the room.

I bought a pair of rubber shoes, the same as everyone else wore. They were extremely comfortable, easy to kick off, and with all the mud and wetness were the only practical thing to wear. They were thick black rubber, stamped from a mold, with a fancy design of shoelaces up the front. They came in all sizes; babies wore them, and the old men over their heavy wool socks and gnarled feet. I always loved to see a pair of these huge men's shoes, dusty and mud-caked, askew on the dirt floor outside a room, surrounded by a swarm of smaller ones, like two patriarchal black ducks swimming in a brood of their ducklings. In the towns you could buy these shoes in bright colours, blue, green, silvery lavender, for the women, but in the villages you could only get them in black.

It was a mystery to me how they always found their own in a heap of sometimes fifty identical shoes kicked off outside a door. Whenever I began to hunt for mine someone had to come and help me, picking through the pile and infallibly pulling out first one and then the other. Only once did I get someone else's. I was already half-way back to my house when a boy came running, waving another left shoe in his hand. Even so I couldn't really tell the difference, they both had 38 stamped on the bottom and the same design of shoelaces and felt exactly the same on.

*

The days got shorter and suddenly one night there was a howling wind, snow and ice, and I understood what was meant by the bitter desolation of Anatolian winters. However, we were prepared. A few days earlier Elif had woken me up, yelling, '*Kalk, kalk, Muhtar odun getirdi . . .*' I understood as much as, 'Get up, get up, the Muhtar is here with the . . .' and then remembered that *odun* meant 'forest'. A big cartload of wood had been dumped in front of our house and the Muhtar was beginning to hack the logs into smaller pieces. He worked for over an hour and had several little boys carry it bit by bit into the shed behind the house.

When he was finished, he said, 'Let's play cards.'

We stopped by the school, he got Kâmuran out of class and we went on to the Muhtar's house to celebrate the wood and to play *kaptıkaçtı*, their favourite card game. The stake was a chicken, which Hacı İsmail ended up having to buy for Kâmuran. He sent it around to him that afternoon, alive, and Kâmuran kept it for a day tied up in the hallway outside his room, but then he sent it back for İnci, the Muhtar's wife, to cook.

Along with the wood, they installed a tin stove in my room, with a very rickety tin pipe going out a hole in the wall for the ventilation. The stove burned with a roar and turned red hot, and then abruptly went out and within seconds was cold and dead again. Although I always politely stretched out my hands to the stove, the temperature during the day, except for those bursts of roaring heat, was never above 8 or 9 degrees centigrade. I had a big flattish stone that I put in the back of the fireplace in the centre room every day to heat up, and then slid into the bottom of my bed at night. I really loved that stone. Once I got used to not cracking my toes on it, it was like having a little animal, all warm, at the bottom of the bed.

As the weather changed and got colder day by day, the women slowly put on more and more clothing. They did not have special clothes for hot weather or for cold weather. In summer they wore one dress, in winter four or five, pulled on more and more tightly one over the other, or two dresses and three skirts, with numerous sweaters. In the same way, the men wore two or three pairs of trousers over pyjama bottoms when it got really cold, and long knitted scarves around their heads and faces. They borrowed overcoats from each other when they had to go to another village or to Ankara.

All these clothes made them look much heftier than they were, especially the women. I had always thought of Asiye Nedihe as a rather small yet substantial old lady, but one night she came padding through my room looking for something, wearing only a striped cotton shift, and I was astounded to see how frail she really was – about half her usual size during the day.

Everyone in the village loved to have their picture taken, seeming to feel none of the restraint that many Muslims do about being photographed. Only one time, in another village, a young woman turned her face away with disapproval, but she wanted very much a picture of her baby. It was almost impossible to take any spontaneous, candid shots. The minute they saw my camera, they froze in their tracks, even the children standing stiffly to attention, their hands flat along their sides, staring unblinking and totally expressionless at the camera.

Whenever I took a picture of one of the women or her daughter or granddaughter it became a lengthy and complex business. They would put a pillow down on the floor and make me sit on it, saying hectically, '*Dur* ... *dur* ... wait ... wait,' and begin digging into the wooden chest in their sleeping room, pulling out every possible piece of clothing they owned. With neighbour women crowding around they put on first one dress, then over it another, a sweater, a skirt, another sweater, until they had emptied the chest. A series of scarves was draped over their heads and, since they usually had no mirror, they looked in their neighbours' faces and accepted their opinion of what looked best. They finally bulged through the door, and stood ready and smiling in the sun. I pleaded with them to wear just one thing, to keep at least some human shape, only *one* dress or one skirt as that would be all that would be in the picture, but they didn't pay attention. I have a picture of one of the young women, her legs like sticks holding up an enormous bale of clothes. Furthermore she had at the last minute stuffed herself into a pink wool overcoat that her husband had sent her from Germany. The picture was for him and she wanted him to see how nice she looked in all the clothes he had been sending her.

*

Kâmuran claimed that they could not really visualize themselves or really know what they looked like in a picture. He said a son in the army could send a picture of anybody at all in uniform and his parents would tack it proudly on the wall. In the towns, looking at the windows full of photographs of soldiers you could understand this in a way. They posed with plastic flowers held rigidly in front of them, or sitting at a desk with a telephone at one ear, and although the shapes of their heads and features were individual, the external expressions were all the same: vacant poker faces with round eyes staring hollowly into the photographer's lens. When several soldiers posed together, the one in the centre held the flowers and the others tenderly clasped the nearest shoulder with both hands, like old-fashioned postcard valentines. The soldiers seemed to pose with flowers, and the young civilians with guns, either their own or borrowed, cocked in front of their faces or laid against their ears pointing towards the sky. In group pictures, they pointed the guns at each other.

The local photographer of Çorak had his shop near the hotel, and whenever I was there I sat and had tea with him. He would come out of his darkroom with a strip of dripping negatives and go out in the street in front of his shop to finish washing it, holding it up high and pouring a slow stream of water down it from an earthenware jug. The wet prints he laid out on a cloth-covered board which he then deftly slammed up against the inside window pane of his shop and braced with a wooden stick, to dry in the sun.

Towards the end of the school year an ambulant photographer walked into Uzak Köy one morning, as he did every year, to take identification pictures of the children in the last class for their certificates. He had a battered box camera on wooden legs that he had been using for fifty-three years. He charged 1 lira for four little snaps and there was great excitement and running around for the money and posing against the mud wall of the schoolhouse. He developed them on the spot, in chipped enamel trays which he slid under Kâmuran's camp bed out of the light. Something went wrong with one batch and the pictures came out printed as negatives – black faces with white hair and smokey white eye-sockets and noses – but the children snatched them from hand to hand, somehow found their own and ran off cheering.

In the same way suddenly one day a man walked into the village, with an accordion around his neck, and a little black wooden box with a handle. He played a short tune on the accordion several times and sat down on a rock. He was the ambulant circumciser, who also came once a year. I saw Teoman run up to the school and run back dragging Murat, his eleven-year-old son, after him. He waved to me and said I could come and watch and take pictures if I wanted. I didn't understand what was happening but rushed over to Teoman's house anyway. A group of men were squatting on the floor, trying to hold Murat down. They had pulled off his trousers. He was bellowing like an animal, and struggling wildly to get free. The circumciser was kneeling on the ground in front of him. Teoman finally caught Murat's head and covered the boy's eyes with his big rough hands. Two men had caught his legs and were holding them flat on the mud floor. The circumciser had a pair of scissors in one hand, and he hunched up closer and burrowed into the boy's crotch. Murat was screaming in terror. Some women were standing in the background chatting. I tried to take some pictures but my hands were shaking too much and then suddenly my knees gave out. I went over to Murat's mother and simply stood in front of her. She instantly put her arms around me and I burst into tears. They laughed a lot about that later.

Murat was carried into another room, laid on a mat in the corner and covered up. He was crying in long choking sobs. Usually this operation was done when a boy was only a few years old. Teoman year after year had never had the 10 lira to pay the circumciser, until now, and Murat had got older and older. Everyone sat around having tea, ignoring the muffled sobbing of Murat, motionless under the quilt. The circumciser was looking at me resentfully; he had not liked my taking pictures. Maybe he thought I was spying in some way, and he said several times, 'Clean, clean, I do good clean work...' I wasn't about to argue with him about anything at all and only kept repeating one of the phrases I knew, '*Çok güzel, çok güzel,*' which meant very pretty, lovely, and beautiful. He warmed up after a while, and asked me to take his picture. He posed in front of the Muhtar's house, playing his accordion, with a silly smile on his face.

I paid Asiye Nedihe 70 lira a week, about £2.50, for my room. I can't remember how we settled on that amount, I know I could have offered half that and she would have accepted it gladly. It was a tremendous amount of money for them, they had been living on literally nothing, some wheat and flour from her older son, who himself had thirteen people to support in his own family. With the first week's rent they bought rubber shoes, sugar, tea.

Every Saturday morning I handed Asiye Nedihe an envelope with seven 10-lira notes in it. Like a real landlady, she counted the bills, nodded, sniffed, tucked the envelope into her skirts and waddled out to lock it in the wooden chest to which only she had the key. There was no question that she, despite being a very frail old lady, was the head of the household in the absence of her son.

Elif, who loved to talk about money and how much things cost, one night came and sat on the end of my bed. She asked me how much a hotel room cost in Ankara.

'Well, some cost a lot of money, but there are others for about 10 lira a night,' I answered, 'just what I am paying you.'

'How much for one month in Ankara then?'

'Well, either 300 lira or 310, depending on how many days there are in the month.'

She had a crafty look in her eyes. She knew how to count. 'Then you're not paying us as much as you would in a hotel in Ankara.'

'Elif, what are you saying? It's exactly the same, 10 lira a night, *neh*?'

'No! Because if you pay us 70 lira a week, is only 280 lira a month, and that leaves over 2 or 3 days a month you don't pay us anything!'

I was speechless. I could see it was one of those arguments that had absolutely no way of being explained. I got very worked up, even getting out some paper and trying to draw a picture of the months and how the weeks fell, that those two or three days were part of the next week's rent, that some months might have five Saturdays, in which case, according to her, I was paying more than I should, and that if you took a whole year, with 52 weeks at 70 lira week, etc. But she continued to look crafty and unconvinced, and I finally gave up, although for a long time I found myself still trying to think up ways of making her see reason.

Ramazan

It was the beginning of Ramazan. Ramazan is one of the Five Pillars of Islam, the precepts that regulate the overall religious life of a Muslim in his very direct relationship with God. The first pillar is creed, one sentence: 'There is no God but Allah and Mohammad is his Prophet.' This must be said at least once during a man's lifetime, with total submission and understanding, but in practice it is repeated many times a day. The second is prayer. Five times a day, upon rising, at noon, mid-afternoon, after sunset and before sleep, a Muslim must pray. It does not matter where he is. He stops work in a field and kneels on the ground, he goes into a corner of a room full of people, or a free space in a bus station or office and turns his heart and face towards Mecca, the holy city where Islam first became manifest. The third pillar is charity. The Koran is not as interested in why some people have more than others as in what can be done about it. A specific portion of a man's possessions is given annually to those in need. Left-over food is sent daily to the mosque for the poor, or given to beggars who come to the door every evening.

The fourth pillar is fasting during Ramazan, the ninth month in the Arabic calendar, the holy month during which Mohammad first received his momentous revelations through the mouth of the Angel Gabriel, and ten years later made the historic *hegira*, or flight, from Mecca to Medina. Ramazan fasting is a meaningful experience. It teaches self-discipline, it turns the mind inward, it reminds a man of his dependence on Allah and of his own basic weakness despite his pretensions, and most important it revives compassion in his heart. Only if you have been hungry can you know what hunger is, and you will listen more carefully when you are approached by someone in distress. There is a saying in Arabic, 'Hunger that knows it will eat should not be called hunger'. This is true of the Ramazan fasting: you know that the day will end, that you will have food, yet you take it thoughtfully, reflecting on those who have nothing. The fifth pillar is the pilgrimage to Mecca, the *Hadj*, which every Muslim if physically and economically able, must make once in his lifetime. Before entering the sacred precincts the pilgrim takes off his usual clothes with their distinctions of social class and nationality, and puts on a simple white sheet-like garment, to stand with his brothers in undivided equality before Allah.

Ramazan this year began in the middle of November. The time of fasting is from sunrise to sundown, or the moment when you can no longer distinguish a white thread from a black thread. In the cities and towns a cannon is fired before daybreak and in the evening to mark these times. In some villages before dawn a man goes from house to house beating on every door to wake the people for their last meal before the morning light begins to appear. Now, in the month of November, the evening meal was at five o'clock, and the last meal before dawn at four-thirty. As it follows a lunar calendar, Ramazan falls approximately ten days earlier each year. In summer, fasting is more arduous. The hours of daylight are protracted, from three o'clock in the morning until nine o'clock at night sometimes. It is difficult to go without food but especially without water during the burning summer heat and difficult to work in the fields that cannot be neglected. In winter, the days are short. In the villages there is little pressure of work, and you sleep through many of the waiting hours.

In Uzak Köy they had no cannon and no one to make the rounds pounding on the doors. They knew the correct times in the evening from the colour of the sky, but mainly from the prayer on the radio broadcast from the principal mosque in Ankara. I fasted, too. Countless times during those twenty-eight days I was alone in my room and could easily have had a piece of bread or some walnuts, yet the thought never entered my mind. Everyone had asked me if I was going to fast, and when I said yes, I knew from the way they smiled that they were pleased, although I felt they would not have resented it had I not fasted. Some of the older men and women asked me almost every day, 'Are you still fasting?' and they patted me and nodded to each other as if to say, 'You see?'. The younger less devout men asked too but in a more teasing way, as for them it was less important and they knew it was a new thing for me.

In the beginning, apart from a sort of feverish light-headedness, the hardest thing to get used to was the meal in the early morning before sunrise. In my house they did not have a clock and the first few nights Asiye Nedihe got everyone up at two o'clock. Elif and her two oldest girls slept like stones and it took her a long time to wake them up. I would wake up instantly in the dead cold dark, as she began croaking, 'Elif ... Elif ... Selvan ... Fatma...' But on her side of the door nobody moved. She shouted louder a few minutes later, and again and again, until there were groans and mumbles and Elif stumbled out of her covers and kicked the two girls out of their sleep. She banged on my door, 'Get up, get up, come...' Those first mornings I showed them my clock and that it was only two o'clock and that we could all sleep a few more hours before it was time to eat. But they were all up and had started the fire and pushed the pot over towards it.

We finally found a better system. I set my alarm for quarter past four and woke them up myself every morning. I always made as much noise as possible with my door, climbing over them to light their kerosene lamp and shouting all the while, 'Elif! Asiye Nedihe! Selvan!' Most often, nothing happened, nobody moved. After more shouting and prodding, I would usually get a feeling of mild hysteria. I simply couldn't believe they weren't all going to leap out at me any second from under their covers. Asiye Nedihe was always the first to rally, and together we pushed and pulled the others awake and onto their feet. Everyone sat groggily in front of the fire, ate their soup and bread and then got back into their bedding to sleep again. I took whatever I had back into my bed with me and read, although it was difficult, coming out of that warm animal sleep into the icy darkness, to find any real zest for food. I opened the curtain and looked across the village, at the faint light in every house, and I could feel the stirring of a common heart beneath the dark and the cold and the silence.

Every evening during Ramazan there was an invitation to a different house for the main evening meal. The first time Asiye Nedihe and Elif and the children went to join the women at a big party at the Muhtar's house, they didn't get home until nine-thirty, which is like rolling in at three o'clock in the morning. Asiye Nedihe was overexcited and she talked and wheezed and laughed in her bed-roll on the floor for almost an hour. She had brought me a piece of warm soft *lokum* in a little piece of cloth which she had kept all evening inside her shirts between her breasts.

The families who had sufficient food prepared big dinners and invited the poorer men of the village, and always the İmam, the head of the mosque, and Hacı İsmail, the Muhtar and Kâmuran, the Hoca, and now me, as guests. Three or four trays were set out on the floor and twenty-five or thirty men crowded around them. I was the only woman, and at the time I was not really aware of the magnitude of their courtesy and kindness. I was not a Muslim, I was a woman alone, and these two facts were enough to warrant suspicion, disapproval and exclusion.

People sat more or less as they came in, talking or not talking. There was always a radio, their own or a borrowed one, tuned to Radio Ankara, and as the room filled up it became more and more quiet under the chanting from the Ankara mosque. Then a clear strong voice intoned the evening prayer. The fast was ended. Everyone moved up closer around the trays, pulling the cloth over their feet and knees and murmuring the blessing, '*Bismillah*', then picked up a folded piece of limp bread and took a swallow of water from a glass that was passed from hand to hand to open the meal. The head of the family, the host, stood to one side and he and his older son or sons, or sons from a neighbouring house, passed the full dishes and placed them in the centre of each tray. The first dish was always a wheat soup. The wheat is soaked in water, handfuls are taken and rubbed together like a cloth being washed, until the water is milky white, and then it is boiled and sprinkled with dried mint. White beans in a hot red pepper sauce, little balls of wheat in a pale soupy sauce, a sweet pudding of rice and milk and water, then potatoes cut in small pieces simmered in water and oil, a bowl of *pekmez*, the much-loved grape syrup thick like molasses, then layers of bread dough cooked in fat. Water. It was always the same menu with slight variations, a banquet compared to the daily fare of the rest of the year. By the middle of winter not much was left of the small supply of sugar beets, pickled tomatoes or dried grapes that each family put aside from summer, and a single dish of potatoes, beans or boiled wheat was the usual meal, or simply bread with a handful of chopped onions.

Everyone ate quickly and the dishes were taken away while still half-full, to be given to the women in the next room. There was hardly any conversation. Before the end of the meal, the İmam abruptly began a prayer and the men dropped their bread and raised both hands in front of them, palms upward, and murmured the words with him. His prayer was in Arabic, learned by rote a long time ago, the words now unintelligible and their meaning lost, but no one would think to wonder what it meant. When the meal was finished, the trays were lifted away and the men got to their feet and queued up to wash at a tin basin in a corner of the room, where one of the sons held the soap and towel and poured water over their hands. The men spread out and sat in a packed line against three sides of the room. The father or his son swept the floor clean with a short straw broom and went around dropping little tin ashtrays in front of every second person. For a few minutes everyone shifted and moved to get comfortable on their haunches and soon the room began to cloud with cigarette smoke.

Then again without warning the İmam rose and went to stand at the wall facing south. The men rose and formed in lines. In one gesture, they all turned their caps around so that the visor lay in back. The first evening I didn't know what was happening and I stood up too in confusion. Hacı İsmail said, 'You stay. There in back, sit, sit.' There were three rows of eight or nine men and the room suddenly seemed very small. The İmam called out the beginning of the prayer, and instantly all the men in their dark anonymous clothing and matted wool socks full of holes were fused, their shoulders almost touching, into a single obedient body. The act of prayer is a prescribed ritual and the movements never vary. A man stands erect, his hands open at either side of his face and his thumbs on the lobes of his ears as he says the first words: 'Allah is most great'. Still standing, he continues to pray, then bows from the hips with his hands on his knees. He stands upright again, then sinks to his knees and puts his hands and his forehead to the ground. He sits up straight on his heels, then again puts his hands and his forehead to the ground. These movements are repeated several times. The prayer too does not change. It is of praise and gratitude, a simple act of worship, not a petition for favours or a personal dialogue with Allah.

*

All the things I had been reading began to take on meaning. In 1923 one of the dramatic reforms in Kemal Atatürk's secularization of Turkey was the demand that Western hats be worn instead of the fez, which to him was the symbol of Muslim fanaticism. This caused great anguish among pious Muslims, who considered the hat an infidel execration, the brim rightly hiding the shameful pagan face from the sight of God. There were riots and defiance. Atatürk declared the wearing of the fez a criminal offence. Within three weeks, with thousands of Turks hung, beaten or imprisoned, this reform was complete. Besides the more Western appearance it produced, perhaps he hoped that a head under a European hat would think European thoughts. The hat, furthermore, might in an insidious way discourage prayer, as the brim made it difficult to touch the forehead to the ground. But the people got around this by adopting the visored cap, which could be swivelled front to back so the wearer, his head still covered, could easily touch his forehead to the ground while performing the ritual prayer.

Turkey had come so far. Much of the population after the First World War had been lost through battle, disease and starvation. No proper roads existed, only one railway from Istanbul with a few dead-end branches into Anatolia. Malaria and typhoid still broke out. There were no industries, no technicians or skilled workmen, in a country 90 per cent illiterate, with no established government. The heaviest liability, however, of Atatürk's derelict legacy from the Ottoman Empire was the great mass of benighted peasants, rooted in lethargy, living in remote poverty-stricken villages untouched by the outside world. Atatürk was determined to loosen the hold of Islam on the people, which he believed was the major obstacle to modernization, and to awaken a sense of Turkish national pride. He fought fiercely for the emancipation of women, denouncing the veil, giving them the right to vote and to divorce. He had a consuming faith in the qualities and the character of the peasants. The élite of the cities should turn to the people, he said, as the living museums of Turkey's cultural heritage. The élite possessed civilization, the people culture. 'Atatürk understood our country,' Kâmuran always said. 'He was a peasant himself.'

Whenever I quoted facts and figures about how much had been accomplished or still needed to be done, Kâmuran grew impatient. That there were only two taxis and one private car in the entire enormous province of Bingöl in 1963, that in 1962 only 5,000 out of 60,000 religious leaders could write the Latin alphabet, that now nearly 6 million students were registered instead of the 380,000 when his father was his age, that the GNP was rising at a steady 7 per cent a year, did not interest him.

'I do not understand numbers like that, they are not important for us now, maybe later. Only the things that keep these people's minds closed are important now.'

*

The prayer ended and the men went back around the room and sat against the wall. On one of the first evenings I found myself sitting next to the İmam. He was an old man with only two large brown teeth, a big mottled nose, loose unshaven cheeks and a gruff manner. He was not from Uzak Köy and moved from house to house, spending two nights in each, and every family looked forward to their turn to receive him. I was rather afraid of him, as I knew that he, more than anyone in the village, must question my presence with mistrust. He had been very busy the week before talking about the astronauts and Apollo 12's trip to the moon. He had sermonized in his little mud mosque and told the men that they must not believe what was being said, none of it was true, and all the pictures were just fake pictures. He said that a while ago a man had tried to go to the moon, but had been eaten by the big fish that lived in the heavens and protected Allah's domain.

If again someone had tried to enter this sacred region, they also would have been swallowed by this big fish, as big as the moon itself. All this was a wicked endeavour and could only result in terrible punishment.

Even Hacı İsmail, who was really open to the world, was made thoughtful by what the İmam said. We had long slow discussions in Hacı İsmail's house about it, with the older men emphatically agreeing for religious reasons and others agreeing for simple technological reasons. It was so clearly impossible to fly to the moon, all the stars and the big fish in the way were beside the point. Hacı Kadin poked me in the side and asked on her own if it were true that they had gone to the moon, and I uncertainly began to answer, 'Well, yes, I think they did ... but ...' She interrupted in a bewildered soft voice saying only, '*Why?*' I tried to say that they must not worry about these things, that in a few years they would all be a natural part of our lives. Had not electricity and the radio and automobiles been equally unbelievable and thought to be the works of the devil? Allah's world is bigger than anyone knows, and they agreed with this. Kâmuran was left alone to try to explain and he felt his way slowly, slowly, but there was no way to break through and I saw him turning into himself, dicouragement on his face.

So I was feeling mindful of the İmam, and kept my eyes down and my feet under my skirts. When the little glasses of tea were passed around he waved his in my direction, and it was set down in front of me. He sniffed loudly when I thanked him. He was not accustomed to making small talk and, working the heavy folds of his face up into a quivering unaccustomed social smile, he reached out and pinched a corner of my skirts and loudly said, as if he were talking to a child, 'This?' I gave him the name in Turkish, and then the name for my shoe, my arm, my hand, my nose, as he pointed to each in turn, thankful that I had actually learned those words rather in the same way. He pointed to my cigarette. I said, '*Jarra*', which is the local slang name for cigarette, and he slapped his knee and laughed. From then on we were friends, although we never talked about anything complicated, and after he had looked through his Koran to make sure it wasn't a sin, he said I could take his picture if I wanted.

One morning during Ramazan, Asiye Nedihe came scuttling into Kâmuran's school in a very excited state. 'Come, come,' she panted, 'Duran's cow just died. He is selling the meat...' Kâmuran was alarmed and told her that, besides being forbidden by the Koran to eat meat that had not been ritually slaughtered, it was also dangerous to eat the meat of an animal that had died without reason like that; the animal could be sick and you would eat the sick meat and it could make you sick too. But she looked at him with a blank face. *Not* to eat this meat fallen from heaven was unthinkable. After she left, Kâmuran said darkly, 'You wait, we will eat this cow too, whether we want to or not.' It was, of course, a windfall, especially for the festive evening meals of Ramazan. And for seven days in a row, in seven different houses, we ate the cow in all its forms, the muzzle and brains one night, the stomach and intestines another, the liver, the meat and grizzle in stews, the tail, the feet, and at the end of the week we could reconstruct the entire animal as it had passed across our plates. Nobody got sick, and it was the only time in the village that we had meat, except during the great Kurban Bayramı feast which falls twelve weeks after the end of Ramazan, when every family that is able, kills a lamb or a sheep. This most important Muslim celebration is in commemoration of Abraham's sacrifice of his son Ismail. I asked Kâmuran to tell me his version of this sacred story and to my amazement he had nothing to say. He had watched for twenty-two years the ritual killing of a lamb and had never thought to question the origin of the ceremony. Later in New York, I asked a Turkish friend, from a wealthy Istanbul family, the same question. He looked rather vague and said, 'Oh, it's to celebrate when they found the little baby in the river. And then the Prophet Mohammad slaughtered a lamb.' I said, '*What!*' and he brusquely said, 'Well, history has never interested me very much.' I wondered if there were any Christians, even non-believers, who would not know the story behind Christmas or Easter.

Very early one morning, half-way through Ramazan, Emirel, Hacı İsmail's son, came into my room. It was still dark, I had heard a knock and pulled the heavy cotton quilt up over my head and moved over against the wall, which was the only way, I had learned, to keep from being disturbed. Most times, whoever it was would come up to the side of the bed and stand there for a few moments noisily shifting from foot to foot, sometimes lifting up a corner of the quilt hoping to find a shoulder or an arm to poke, but finding only an unresponsive back, would get discouraged and go away with a sigh. Emirel, though, nudged so insistently that I had to turn over and he said urgently, 'Come, come, my father wants to see you.'

Getting up for them was simply a matter of rolling over and getting up. Most of them slept half dressed, in one or two layers of clothing, and had only to pull on a pair of extra trousers or another skirt, reach out for their cap or rewind a scarf around their uncombed hair. I told Emirel rather testily that I would come but he would have to wait, and he went outside. Then I got a little worried and wondered if anything serious was the matter.

When we got to the Muhtar's house, the kerosene lamp was brightly lit and Hacı İsmail was still in his bed, with his cap on, lying back on his bedding on the floor. He thought he had a fever, and he knew he had a very bad headache. I gave him two analgesic tablets, a supply of which I always carried in my pocket, and got him a glass of water from the bucket in the corner. He started to put the tablets under his pillow and I said, 'No, you must take them now, with a lot of water. In ten minutes your headache will go.' But it was Ramazan, and he was not allowed to take even a swallow of water. 'Tonight, I'll take them tonight, when I'm better,' he said, patting the pillow. Then he said, looking at me without blinking, 'Let's play cards.'

I smiled to myself the whole rest of the morning. It isn't against the Koran to take water during Ramazan if you are ill; it is against the Koran to play cards, but I guessed he knew all that much better than I did.

Everyone agreed that the hardest thing to do without was cigarettes. All the men smoked a great deal. Whenever you met someone or went into a house cigarettes were offered almost before the greetings were finished. One pack would be passed around the room and emptied before it got back to you, but since everyone contributed their share it always seemed to work out fairly enough. Hacı İsmail was an unconventional man, and he tossed cigarettes around the room willy-nilly into people's laps. In the poorer houses that had no carpets you flipped the butts into a corner, but where there were carpets little tin ashtrays cut out of old tin cans were always spread around the floor by your feet.

The older women smoked too, and when there was a party or a gathering with all the women talking together in one of the rooms, Hacı İsmail would stick his face in and throw a pack of cigarettes into their midst. The women smoked deliberately and slowly, following the white curls of smoke with half-closed eyes, holding the cigarette pinched between the broken yellowed nails of their thumb and first finger in a very worldly fashion. They didn't know about inhaling, and when you lit their cigarettes there was always a flurry of sparks as they concentrated on blowing out. To get rid of the ash they gently pressed a finger against the end of the cigarette.

On a trip to Ankara I had obtained a huge brown glass ashtray from a friend who worked in one of the big hotels to bring back as a souvenir for Hacı İsmail. It had indentations around the edge for six cigarettes, and

I thought it would be ideal for his card-playing hours. I gave it to him, explaining where it had come from and that I had more or less begged it for him. He laughed and turned it over, very pleased, several times in his hands, said that it was very beautiful, *çok güzel*, and then he looked at me with narrowed eyes and said, 'What is it?'

As Kâmuran and I had been invited every night to someone's house I asked him if he did not want in turn to offer a meal one evening before the end of Ramazan. He did not really know how to cook, and his room was too small to hold more than five or six people, but he loved the idea and I told him I would do all the cooking if he gave me a day's notice. We went over the menu and talked about the men he wanted to invite, and we set the day for when we had got together ten or more eggs. It was late November and the chickens had stopped laying, so this was a problem; also there was no yoghurt or milk any more, but I was determined to make my menu as I wanted to prepare things for them they had never tasted.

I told Asiye Nedihe and Elif about these plans and they were pleased and excited. They asked what pots I would need and offered their spoons, and said that everything must be neat and clean. Asiye Nedihe was all for it, and I woke up at night plotting out the various dishes and how I could get them cooked in the right order on just one little kerosene stove. I saw that synchronization would take up most of the time. Every morning I said to Kâmuran, 'Eggs? The eggs?' and he answered, 'Maybe tomorrow.' He had made the announcement in his classroom and there was nothing to do except wait.

When the time came, I was going to buy a chicken for 10 lira from Bekir next door, and I had the six remaining carrots and five leeks from a batch Kâmuran had bought in Çorak two weeks earlier. I was going to make a leek soup, a huge potato omelet, a chicken stew with carrots, rice pudding with walnuts and an apricot compote, and had figured out more or less exactly how and when to cook each thing during the day so they would all be ready by five o'clock. By Thursday only four eggs had come in and Kâmuran said the omelet was a bad idea as Ramazan would be over by the time we got the rest, but I said let's wait and who knows.

I was working in my room Friday afternoon and as usual at three o'clock the school let out and the children came running and shouting past the window. Suddenly Kâmuran appeared at the door. 'Come, come. They are coming tonight. You must cook.'

'Kâmuran! MY DINNER! It's three-thirty! I can't cook all those things by five o'clock! It can't be done, oh my God...' I wailed.

'Yes, come, come, don't worry, you can cook.'

I rushed to get Asiye Nedihe to tell her what had happened and she moaned, '*Aman... aman...*'

Kâmuran was out the door, 'I put the table, you cook.'

Bahri was walking by and I yelled at him to go next door, find the chicken, kill it, and get its feathers off. Asiye Nedihe was already piling up pots and pans. I could hear Bahri running outside and the terrible squawking of a chicken vigorously trying to escape. He brought it to the school a few minutes later, a fleshless, pale mauve little carcass with incredibly long thin legs and a long thin neck dangling from its puckered bony body. Elif came to the window of Kâmuran's room, looking upset. She went off to borrow another kerosene cooker and Bahri filled up the little tin stove in the middle of the room with wood and chunks of dried dung and lit it. Kâmuran's water buckets were empty. Halil and Yunus, left over from school and standing intensely by, grabbed them and ran out to the fountain on the other side of the village. I hacked away at the carrots and put them with the chicken on the kerosene stove and the apricots on top of the tin stove. Elif came back with the second kerosene cooker and we wordlessly got it going out in the hall on the floor. I put the rice on that. I hated to give up the omelet but with only four eggs it seemed out of the question, so I cut up the potatoes for the soup. It was getting dark and the room was stifling and full of steam. I had to use a torch when I went out into the hall to stir the rice and prime the stove every few minutes. Kâmuran had dragged out his wooden desk to set up in the schoolroom next door, with newspapers neatly spread over it as a table-cloth, and had pulled three school benches around it. Every time he looked into his room he laughed and said, 'Good, good. You see?' Once I caught a glimpse of Asiye Nedihe hovering in the dark hall outside wringing her hands.

It was quarter to five. The chicken suddenly smelled as if it were cooked, the apricots began to puff up and the rice started to look soupy. I felt a deep sigh well up from my lungs and a great wave of calm descend, as if the next thirty minutes were all the time in the world. The soup was also beginning to boil, and I blew on the hot chicken and on my fingers as I tore off the tough shreds of meat and put them back with the carrots. A boy came in with a load of bread wrapped in a towel. Halil came in walking carefully, balancing an old dented tray with tea glasses and saucers and little tin spoons, something I had not remembered. Kâmuran came to get his transistor radio from its nail over his desk and take it into the schoolroom. The table was ready and looked fine, with wooden spoons laid out and piles of bread at each place and in the centre a little saucer with salt in it. He had borrowed one of the big German kerosene lamps and had lit the stove and the room was bright and warm. The frenzy of cooking at my end had receded and one by one I could put the things in their big enamel bowls and line them up on the floor in the hallway.

A little before five o'clock the men began to arrive and their voices came muffled through the wall. Twelve men had come instead of five or six, and they laughed as they tried to fit onto the low teetering benches. Then there was silence and I knew the prayer had come over the radio and that they had begun to eat. Hacı İsmail had brought another chicken, which was a relief. I carried in all the other dishes and put them out on the table. They had left some soup in the bottom of the bowl, which was for me. They left a corner of food in every other dish too, and Hacı İsmail wrapped a chicken leg in a piece of bread and brought it out to me.

They sat for a long time, talking in the next room, and then came into Kâmuran's room one by one, stepping over the cooking debris, swivelling their caps front to back. They went into the corner, facing the wall, and began their prayer, as there was no space for this in the classroom.

Asiye Nedihe and Elif and the children were waiting for all the news, and when I got home we went over every detail from beginning to end, sitting in a heap together in front of the fire. Asiye Nedihe and I shared cigarettes as usual. She took my hands and, turning each one over near the light, began clucking and exclaiming. There were cuts and hacks and burn blisters over both hands, and dried bits of potato peel and carrot skin hanging all over my sweater sleeves. She pulled my head down on her lap and rocked me back and forth, laughing and sniffling.

Elif's Baby

It was the middle of November and Elif's baby was coming. Just after sunset, she went out in her bare feet and stood heavily in front of the door, shouting for Meryem in the next house. Then she came into my room and said, 'Sit, come and sit.' They put some pillows down and Meryem and I settled on the floor against the wall near the fire and we smoked cigarettes while Elif walked up and down in front of us, rubbing the sides of her enormous belly. She lay down from time to time on the mat on the floor, where Asiye Nedihe, Selvan, Fatma, Pakise and Ekrem were already sleeping under the heavy quilts pulled up over their heads. She made fast sharp whistling noises between her teeth when the contractions were bad. We sat and talked and smoked. Meryem had brought her own baby, Nepuria, and she nursed it until it was asleep and then laid it in a corner. The hours went by; we dozed, and waited. Elif had covered me with my coat while I was half asleep propped against the hard straw pillow. Everything was quiet: ten immobile forms on the mud floor of the small mud room. The old kerosene lamp hung high on the mud wall, spreading its faint shadowed light over the becalmed hours of the slowly-breathing room, holding it in amber.

About five o'clock Elif got up again and woke the others. Stumbling and muttering they dragged their bedding into my room next door, spread the mats and quilts out over the floor again and reassembled in the thick warmth of their sleep. Meryem was hunting through the odds and ends in the bottom of a little niche in the wall, looking for something. She made a gesture up and down her cheek: she needed a *jilet*. I gave her one of my own new razor blades and she tucked it in the folds of her head scarf. Two young neighbour women had come, and were sweeping more straw into the fire. Elif was pacing up and down. They tried to make her come closer to the flames but she was too distressed to pay attention to them. Meryem had kicked together a pile of sand in the corner near the fire, not even sand, but dirt that they had scraped up from in front of the house. Suddenly Elif came over to the pile of sand and lifted up her skirts, the same skirts she had been wearing since I first came to their house months earlier. She squatted down clumsily over the sand, her knees wide apart. Meryem squatted behind her and the two younger women came to either side and, holding her shoulders with one hand, with the other they rubbed forcefully again and again down the broad muscles of her back. Elif pushed them away, stood up and lurched from side to side a few steps and then came back and squatted again. The two women closed around her, one of them clamping her hand over Elif's open up-turned mouth. I was standing helplessly in front of her and she clawed out and almost pulled me over. She was shuddering and straining backwards and the women were pushing down, pushing down the length of her back. The four of us were locked together, rocked back and forth in the rage of her quaking muscles. They talked to her, tensely and out of breath. Meryem was holding a piece of old blue cloth under Elif which she pulled out and looked at from time to time. Elif was snarling with impatience and pain, and again we were clamped in the jaws of her spasm and struggled to keep our balance.

Two more surging wrestling convulsions, with Meryem shouting out quicker and quicker, 'Ha! Ha! Ha!' and suddenly there was a louder shout and Meryem crouched down lower and the baby lay half on the cloth and half in the sand, in a slimy mass of blue-white cord. '*Oğlu!* ... a boy!' she cried. With her thumb and forefinger she squeezed a place flat in the cord and cut it through with the razor blade. A thick spurt of black blood fell into the sand, and she tied the cord with a small piece of string from her pocket. She carefully wiped the razor blade on her skirt and put it back in a fold of her scarf to take home with her. Elif was sagging between us. She caught her breath again and the afterbirth slithered onto the sand. She unsteadily hoisted herself up to her feet. One of the women brushed sand over this last dark mass and kicked it into the corner with her foot. One of the dogs ate it the next morning when the room was cleaned out and everything was swept back out in front of the house.

Meryem had wrapped the baby, his little body coated

with sand and mucus, in the piece of old cloth and had laid him in the big sieve they used for sifting out goat dung from the straw, then had pushed him over near the fire. The two young women pulled Elif's bedding towards the fire too, and in the centre of her mat they poured sand which had been warming in a tin basin on the fire. They carefully spread out the sand, smoothed it down and picked out all the rough pieces of stone and dirt. Elif twisted her skirts around her waist and lay painfully down on the sand. With a great sense of purpose I had gone to boil water in my little blue enamel tea-kettle, but I certainly couldn't remember why. They all looked blank when I shakily held out the steaming kettle in the direction of Elif and the baby. But then Meryem, pleased, said, 'Oh good, good. You are making tea.' So I made tea, passing around the glasses on the battered tray with the scratched picture of the Sophia mosque on it. Elif was leaning on her elbow, chewing on a rolled-up piece of bread and onion and sipping from the glass she had put on the floor beside her.

There had not been a sound from the sieve, but the cloth moved from time to time in short twitches. Meryem had heated some water in the large basin they had used the day before to cook cabbage in and when it was warm enough she pulled it off the fire and on her haunches reached back and pulled the sieve towards her. She unwrapped the baby and holding him on his stomach in her great rough hand began to wash him, scratching loose the crust of sand and scum from his little round head and back with her fingernails. The other women were working over a ragged piece of cotton which they had shaken and laid flat on the floor. In the centre they put more warm sand and meticulously picked it clean and smooth. Meryem laid the baby down in the sand and they carefully lifted his genitals from between his legs, pulled his legs down straight and pressed them flat and tight together. They pulled his arms down flat against his sides, poured a stream of sand on his genitals and wound him up tightly in the cloth. Then another piece of cloth and finally a longer one that they wrapped around him twice and tied with a long strip of cotton which they criss-crossed around him from head to toe until he became a compact little bundle. He would be kept like this for several months to make sure his limbs grew straight. They laid him up in the far corner of Elif's bedding and he was forgotten.

The next morning, dragging in a big basin of warm water, naked and white and shivering in the cold, Elif washed in the corner of my room. She had a tiny cotton rag that she used as a washcloth and another piece of cotton as a towel. The clotted lumps of sand and blood were regularly picked out of her bed and fresh sand, warm from the fire, was put down. The baby was changed in exactly the same way two or three times a day. The village women came to visit. Döndü brought some butter, a wooden spoonful of butter that she carried in a fold of her tucked-up skirt. No one really came to look at the baby, no one seemed much interested. His name would be Ramazan, after the holy month in which he was born.

I had rushed in the morning to the school to tell Kâmuran, and I said eagerly, 'Come and see him, he is beautiful.'

Kâmuran looked startled, then said, 'No. You must learn. This is not something for the men.'

Yusuf

Yusuf was one of the three shepherds of the village and one of the poorest men. He had some 200 sheep to take out at dawn and bring back at sunset, leading them far over the hills to search endlessly for food in the near barren ground. At night, when it was not too cold, many of the sheep slept out in front of his house, and my house next door. I would wade through a sea of pale blurred shapes up to my door, the sheep sighing and coughing, like a person, and throughout the night I could hear a gentle, half-human stirring and breathing outside the window.

Yusuf was paid 2 lira a sheep every six months, that is about 15 pence a sheep for six months' care. I was telling this to someone who had never been to Turkey, and he commented, saying, 'Well, after all, that not's so bad, 15 pence a day...'

Yusuf was a silent man, very thin, his face dark from the sun and unshaven, and he was not very close to the other people in the village. He had his own thoughts and more work than the others during the five winter months. The shepherds seemed the only ones who kept working through those long fallow seasons, and they followed their own rhythm of life. Bekir, one of the other shepherds, was also quite introverted, but younger and more ingenuous than Yusuf. Yusuf rarely visited other houses. When he did he came through the door unsmiling, greeted everyone around the room, stood in the back for a few moments, and then as unsmilingly left. Hardly anyone came to his house. Almost every night however he went to the school to see Kâmuran, coming to the door and stopping to cough to announce his presence and then to knock, toc toc toc, with one finger. Every night the same greeting, the same offering of tea and cigarettes.

'Oh, Yusuf, welcome, good evening. Where have you come from, where are you going? Please sit and tell us.'

He would kick off his shoes and go to sit on the mat in the corner. He stayed for hours, playing with the little transistor radio, smoking, dozing, talking. Here he talked, in a self-absorbed voice, and Kâmuran continued working at his ramshackle desk in the dim light, and Yusuf talked on. Kâmuran did not listen really, but made listening sounds from time to time, 'Mmmm... mm...' and Yusuf talked on. He remembered very clearly when he was a soldier a long time ago, and how cold it had been, how there had been so much vermin and insects and sickness, and how they had taught him to read and write. It was the only time he had been out of the village, and he remembered the name of every town and spot where they had stopped.

'Was life different then?' I asked him once. 'Was it more difficult, was it better?'

'Oh, it is better now. Here in our village it is much better now. Before it was bad, we were afraid to go anywhere, there were always bandits. Now it is safe, we go anywhere. Now it is good.'

Yusuf had eight children. He had recently taken Küçük, who was thirteen, to Ankara and found him a job as a tailor's apprentice. It sounded like a good job and Yusuf and Meryem were happy about it. In a few years he would be earning enough to be able to send some money home. I was soon going to Ankara again and promised to go and see Küçük, and Yusuf with a pencil stub slowly printed out his address on a piece of torn paper.

Küçük was one of my favourite children in the village. He was a smiling shadow behind the others. Among the endless questions they asked me was what my father's name was, what my mother's name was. It was a game, my father's name was Michael, my mother's Paula, and they repeated the funny words but could never remember them. One night walking home in the dark, Küçük was suddenly walking beside me and he said, 'Your father's name is Michael!' and I could see his shy smile through the darkness.

He was working in an old section of Ankara called Ulus. One of the central open markets is here and around it countless small streets and narrow shops selling food and pots and pans and records and materials and perfumes, the displays piled out onto the streets, banked up against the shop fronts, already half-hidden by fantastic bunches of shoes and plastic toys and leather belts swinging in front of the entrances. The street of jewellers blazed like an ocean liner, with huge light bulbs strung along their windows reflecting gold and silver with dazzling brilliance. There were city blocks of wooden stalls, networks of inner passages where you leave the sidewalk and continue along muffled corridors of open shops, like little three-walled rooms, stacked with shelves and boxes of underwear and baby clothes, towels and dishes up to the ceiling, and hung with clothes and hangers and things tied in clusters on wires. If you didn't find what you wanted they sent you with a boy to another shop.

From these crowded noisy streets some wide steps led down into an even older and poorer section, which looked like a village of its own. The narrow streets were in disorder, unpaved or paved with cobblestones, and running with mud and refuse. Dusty ropes of dried okra hung outside the food shops, crates of oranges, wilted lettuce and blotchy vegetables, boxes of hard-boiled eggs dyed bright pink, large tin drums of white cheese floating in a cloudy liquid, hairy goatskin pouches bulging with another kind of white cheese; soap and bread side by side. The butcher's shop windows were packed solid with white lamb carcasses hung in a row, the fat waxy tails pressed flat against the window pane. Clotted sawdust covered the floors. The streets were full of people, women and children too, buying, selling, laughing, sitting on crates talking. Cars did not pass here, except perhaps a delivery van from time to time, honking and inching its way through the confusion.

The houses were two or three storeys high, with

faded peeling grey or khaki or blue walls, unfinished entrance ways, the rough wooden door fitted unevenly on their hinges, broken windows stuffed with newspaper, small dark workshops, thin strips of sidewalk of loose stones or cracked cement. I was sad that it was still only the beginning of spring, because I had seen the sleeping roots and naked branches of wisteria gripping the rutted walls, and over many of the shops were trellises braided with thin winter-brown vines, and in almost all the windows rows of old oil cans sprouting barren twigs. It must be a different world in summer, when there is no mud and vegetables are fresh and cheap, when everything is overlaid with clear bright colours and the warm smell of flowers and leaves.

I found the tailor's shop, down one of these cramped utterly bleak streets. It was a large single room and very dark. Through the window I could vaguely see four men hunched over sewing machines, roughly pulling along the cloth, one sewing on pockets, one zippers, and piling the finished trousers in a heap on the floor. The door to the street opened and a small figure came out. It was Küçük and yet I did not recognize him. In Uzak Köy he was tall and slim, his head shaved and his sweet face tanned, and he had seemed almost a man. Now I thought, 'Who is this small pale child?' He was stuffed into a shabby dark suit, his head covered with thick black hair and his face puffy and white. He looked at me with an expression of distress, as if he didn't recognize me either, or didn't want to see me. I began to give him the greetings of his family and for a flashing second he smiled and I found him again. One of the men came out of the shop, beckoned to me and sent Küçük for tea. I sat near the door. The men did not stop working. Küçük came in with the tea and put it on the window-ledge in silence. Then he went and stood against the wall in the corner, and it was hard to imagine what work he did besides pick up the finished trousers and fold them into another corner, sweep up the cuttings and stand thus in mute blankness through the hours of the day.

I said goodbye and thanked them for the tea and there was a passing nod from each of the men. Küçük came with me to see another boy from Uzak Köy who was working in a small restaurant in a different part of Ulus. We crossed a few busy streets, Küçük leading the way, walking sideways, looking over his shoulder every few steps with his forehead wrinkled, as if he were expecting to be run over or jumped on from behind. He had not said a word so far and at the corner I left him, handing him a package of rice and sugar and walnuts I had bought.

'No, no, I don't want it,' he said.

'Yes, of course, please take it. It's for you.'

He shook his head again, but then took the package without a smile. I wanted to take his face in my hands.

'Are you all right, Küçük? Ankara is so big, do you want to come back to Uzak Köy? Do you want to come home?'

'No, no,' he said, 'Ankara is good.'

Tolay

Yusuf had a dog named Tolay. He was a big, strong, young dog, with short thick grey fur, a square head and round eyes the colour of little oranges, and no ears. They cut off the dogs' ears when they are puppies so they won't lose them later when they are older and begin to get into fights. During the first days, when Tolay saw me he sailed up ferociously, snarling and barking and lunging for my ankles. I just managed to jump clear up to our door. Asiye Nedihe gave me pieces of old bread, 'Here ... now go slowly, slowly, *yavaş, yavaş ...*' and pushed me back through the door. I went out several times with the bread, throwing him pieces which he bolted down. Tolay came for me every time but finally came close enough to tear the bread from my hand and go a few steps back to gulp it down, The next few days he pranced up fiercely again, but looked more towards my hands than my ankles. All the time I talked to him, whispered to him, calling him valiant and good and beautiful. Then one morning there suddenly seemed to be an invisible circle around me, which, with all his feinting, he somehow could not penetrate. He tried to get closer and raised a great deal of dust with his springing and crouching and wheeling, and I suddenly thought I heard a lovely new sound in his impatient growl. Why, you are a big fake, I thought, with all this fuss you are creating around you. You are dying to be loved, and you don't know how to go about it. A day later his tender heart burst open and he stood very still and quivering as I scratched his chest and talked into the scalloped fur edges of his non-existent ears. Whenever he saw me then he would come running, shimmying all the way, and singing out in a high strangled yodel. He would sit on my foot and lean all his weight against me, his eyes half-closed and simple-witted with pleasure.

I was out walking once along the top of a hill overlooking the village and I saw Yusuf and his sheep and Tolay way down in the stony river bed slowly coming home. I called and waved and Tolay broke away and headed up the long steep slope. It was a good half-mile run and I tried to wave him back but up and up he bounded. I had nothing to give him but he did not even sniff at my hands, and we sat for a moment looking at the sunset while he manfully got his breath back. Then we turned home too and whenever I looked down at him he caught my look and answered with a few cake-walk steps, a shake of his head and a snuffle as if to say, 'Yes, yes, yes, we are here, and everything is how it should be.' He was a whole-souled gallant character and we walked for many miles like this, and on several occasions he chased off unfamiliar dogs belonging to shepherds from another village.

Tolay in his new-found friendship, however, could

be exasperating. Whenever I visited Kâmuran, he would sit patiently for hours in the dark hall outside Kâmuran's room and whenever anyone went in he hurtled through their legs and feet and instantly created chaos in the tiny space around the tin stove. He would sniff his way around the room just in case there was something to eat, and then would lie down heavily and beat up a thick cloud of dust with his tail, putting his head between his paws and sighing deeply. With a bluster of threats Kâmuran raised his arm and pushed him with his foot, but Tolay knew it was bluff and steadily beat up more dust. The only way to move him was to pick him up under his forelegs and tow him across the floor out of the room. Tolay would go limp and make himself heavy like a sandbag, and with resignation allow himself to be dragged outside, and then we would hear his tail outside against the door, thump, thump, thump.

Almost every house had a dog of some sort, but not as pets. They guarded the animals and houses, kept away the wolves that appeared in winter. When a stranger walked through the village the dogs skidded up in attacking rows to hurry him past their immediate domain. They were really quite savage and you got by them by skimming stones at them and often an enraged seething snarl turned into piercing heart-rending yelping as a dog retreated holding up a dangling paw or dragging an injured hind leg.

*

In this place where animals had no identity, it greatly amused the Muhtar that anyone should actually talk to a dog or about a dog and call him by name. One afternoon in Hacı İsmail's house someone came through with some letters. There was a letter for me and I put it in my skirt pocket, but everyone was watching and Hacı Kadin said, 'Open it.' There was a photograph inside and that caught the attention even more. Hacı Kadin leaned over to have a look. The letter was from friends of mine in Tangier and the picture was of their little black dog in some snow. Hacı Kadin took the picture and held it upside down and said, 'What is it?' I righted it and said, 'It's a little dog I know.' She turned and stared at me without a word and I had the wild feeling that she for a moment thought that the dog had also written the letter. They passed the picture around and unblinkingly each man explained to his neighbour, 'It's a *dog*.'

With time, Hacı İsmail's imagination was caught and when he wanted to tease someone he pushed him in the ribs and said in his brusque way, 'Eh, Tolay!' or when anyone told a story about somebody else he chuckled and said, 'A real Tolay!' It became a pet name for a lot of people. One day Tolay bit Asiye Nedihe in the ankle, right through her long bloomers and her dark blue socks. We never understood what momentary derangement made him do this, as he had lived next door all his life in a most amiable fashion. It gave Asiye Nedihe a considerable shock, but with Tolay's standing in the community she ended up quite enjoying the experience.

Travelling

'What time will we go?' I asked.

'Four, five, six o'clock,' Hacı İsmail answered.

'Well, which, four, five or six?'

'You can sleep until four,' said Kâmuran.

I set my alarm clock for three-thirty to make sure, but woke up at three. It was pitch dark, no moon, and very cold. I got dressed, shivering, heated some water for tea and wrapped a few walnuts into a piece of bread. On the other side of the village someone began to blast the horn of the tractor standing outside the Muhtar's house. It echoed loudly in the silence. At the same moment, Kâmuran scratched on the window.

'They are waiting for us. Come.'

I put my bread in a piece of cloth and into my basket, and blew out the kerosene lamp. In the next room in the dark I had to feel my way along the wall, slowly stepping through the bedclothes and sleeping forms that covered the floor. The front door creaked on its hinges, a gust of icy air blew in across the floor and Asiye Nedihe grunted in her sleep. Kâmuran was waiting outside and we walked through the mud to the Muhtar's house. For warmth, Kâmuran had folded a piece of newspaper under his little knitted cap pulled over his ears, and put sheets of newspaper under his shirt against his back and chest. It crackled as he moved. 'Better than fur,' he laughed, 'but more noise.'

There were many men already in the main room of the Muhtar's house. The kerosene lamp from Germany was hissing, hanging brilliantly from a beam in the ceiling. They had had numerous guests that night, men from other villages who wanted to make use of this tractor going towards Çorak. The floor was entirely covered with bedding. Four or five men were still lying back among the thick quilts, all with their caps on. Several others in long overcoats were sitting on their haunches against the wall, waiting. Hacı İsmail was near the door, squatting in front of a metal bowl of hot water, with a small mirror propped against the ledge, shaving. Emirel, Hacı İsmail's son, had made tea and was efficiently stepping through the piles of bedding and feet to lift over the huge tin tray. He set it down on its short legs in the centre of the floor within reach of everyone. He poured out little glasses of tea and put down a paper bag of limp biscuits. Hacı İsmail pulled on pyjama bottoms over his trousers, then over the pyjama bottoms another pair of trousers. Everyone was chatting and laughing, the room was glowing and in disorder, the windows black and shiny with night. I sat on one of the wool quilts, still warm from someone's sleep, and had tea and my bread.

'Let us go,' said Hacı İsmail. He waved goodbye over his shoulder to those who were still in bed.

Several more men had gathered outside around the

tractor and the open trailer hooked behind it. The floor of the trailer was covered with a crust of ice. Someone had scattered straw over it and pushed some sacks around the sides against the boards to sit on. Ali Osman, one of the older men, came through the dark with Döndü, his neighbour, following him. She was one of the sad people of the village. Two years ago, her husband, Asiye Nedihe's son, had killed his brother while they were working in their field. There had been a sudden argument about who should go and get food, and it went to the brother's head. He got a gun, came back to the field and shot Döndü's husband. She was a frail, frightened woman, with five small children. She always carried one straddled on her back and pulled along two others clinging to the folds of her skirts. She stood in her doorway, mutely watching people walk by her empty house. She had been ill for several weeks but there had been no chance to get out of the village because of the mud and her condition was not desperate enough to risk the trip on donkeys. Someone had loaned her a man's overcoat and she carried it now folded up in her arms. She was embarrassed and only put it on as we were climbing into the trailer. She and I sat together against the back boards. She was shivering and had put on the coat clumsily, the sleeves pulled down unevenly and the front not closed.

'Cold, cold,' she whispered. I pulled her against me and put my arm around her and Hacı İsmail shifted over so that we could sit sideways out of the full rush of the wind. Salih was sitting across from us, completely encased in a shaggy wool cloak of matted lambskins.

He began to sing, words he made up as he went along, about being a little bird that couldn't find its nest, about his wife having a terrible husband. Everyone laughed. He sang with such enthusiasm and rhythm that most of the men began to clap and croak out the refrain in between coughs and gasps from cold throats and stiff faces.

The trailer bounced over the frozen crests of the rutted road, slowly tilted and slid and manoeuvred across the frozen mud of the inclines. The stars were very close and clear and the round snow-covered hills dimly waded past us, shapeless and brooding in their dark winter isolation.

An hour later we came to the next village, four kilometres away, and stopped at the İmam's house, and crowded into the room. The İmam was sitting up in his bedding on the floor in the far corner and his two grown sons were going about making tea. Everyone found a place to sit along the wall and two chairs were brought for Döndü and me. She had taken off the old overcoat and was carrying it again. She was trembling and I asked her how she was feeling. She had enough strength to look up but not enough strength to clear her throat. She made a few hoarse sounds and an awkward gesture with her hand and I didn't understand what she had said.

From here the road was higher and easier and we went on in two jeeps the remaining forty kilometres to Çorak. Four of us sat in the front seat. The back of the jeep was solid with men and baskets and bundles. The sky was beginning to lighten and we could see each other's faces now. Döndü was on my right, pressed against the canvas door flaps, the sleeves of her coat hanging below her hands and the collar almost engulfing her head. She suddenly shuddered and pitched over onto my lap and pulled the fringe of her scarf over her face. I struggled to get my small pillow out of my basket and put it on my knees under her head. I felt her slowly getting heavier. I was glad to be there. A woman's ailments belonged to the women, a man's to the men, no words were wasted on mutual commiserations and none was expected. I had seen Hacı İsmail stamping through the snow to bring Kâmuran some onions in a piece of newspaper when he was sick, make tea for him, sit with him for many hours during the day. I myself knew the kindness and concern of the women who came to sit on my bed when I was sick. But in general, in public especially, a person's illness was not a subject of interest and it was suffered in silence. A few weeks earlier on the bus to Çorak a man was taking his wife to the dentist. Her jaw was grossly swollen and she was rolling her eyes with pain and cold. Her husband sat her down on one of the rickety metal seats in the middle of the bus and went up to sit with the driver. During the two-hour trip the woman was having what seemed like convulsions, hitting her head against the frozen window. Her husband, in good company up in front, was smoking and talking. When the bus stopped he beckoned to her and she followed him down the street to the dentist's office.

We got to Çorak around eight in the morning, and went to a *lokanta* for breakfast, soup and bread.

Döndü said she didn't want anything, but Kâmuran ordered some soup for her anyway. She sat down and twisted her chair away from the table and tried to take a few spoonfuls of soup, but her hand was trembling and it spilled on the floor and on her lap. Kâmuran told her to push her chair up to the table and bring the plate closer to the edge, but she could only shake her head and look down at her hands, one of them clutching the spoon.

Several of us were going on to Ankara and we went next door to the bus company office and bought tickets for the nine o'clock bus. It was already nine-fifteen and we sat down to wait among the bales of wool and brooms and bags of wheat piled around the red-hot stove. Ali Osman came in shortly with Döndü. Her teeth were chattering and she was waxy pale. Kâmuran made her sit near the fire. I asked when she was going to see the doctor; she had already been. He had given her an injection and Ali Osman said she would be all right now. Kâmuran was watching her. He abruptly took her arm and said, 'You must lie down, I will find a bed for you at the hotel until you go back. Come.'

'No, no,' said Döndü.

'Come,' said Kâmuran almost angrily, looking around at the others, and she followed him out. No one noticed them leave.

'When is the bus going, do you think?' I asked nobody in particular. I was looking forward to the trip.

'Maybe ten, maybe eleven, when it gets here we will know when it leaves.' Everyone laughed.

*

Most Turkish buses are huge, modern German-made coaches, with reclining seats, little curtains and ear-shattering radios. The drivers are businesslike. There are only good drivers in Turkey, they say, all the bad drivers are already dead. Every driver has his subordinate, usually a young boy in shabby clothes and of unquenchable good humour. It is his job to pile on the luggage, get everything tied in place, leap from the front door to the back if anyone wants to get on or off. He hands out small bottles of water from a box under the dashboard and sweeps up the orange peelings and nutshells. Every hour he goes down the aisle with hard candies or chewing gum in a cardboard box, and from a huge bottle of cologne he spurts a pool into each pair of cupped outstretched hands. You rub your hands together, bury your nose and inhale deeply, and then wipe your hands dry over your face and hair. He passes out the plastic bags, as getting car-sick is an uninhibited occurrence, even on dead straight roads. On the more provincial buses where plastic bags are a luxury, a big empty oil can is set on the bottom step of the rear exit and you queue up as best you can. Usually the women simply snap their knees open and are sick between them on the floor. During the stops at the *lokanta*, their husbands make them eat, and the same thing promptly happens all over again. The general atmosphere nevertheless is festive. Food and cigarettes and babies are handed around and small groups form around the bus driver to brighten his trip.

The first time I took a bus from Istanbul to Ankara I was staying at a small hotel in Sirkeci, and they got me a bus ticket from a company that belonged to the brother of the hotel manager. The bus was a time-worn, ramshackle machine, with cracked window panes and the windscreen almost totally obscured by faded plastic flowers and pipal leaves agonizingly entwining pea-green cotton canaries. Huge plastic letters dangled across the entire front, spelling out TRUST IN GOD in Turkish. The seat next to the driver had come unscrewed from the floor and rocked over against the door every time we went around a curve. Grey crumbs of foam rubber were coming out of invisible tears in almost every seat. Even the driver's assistant seemed disenchanted. Older, too, somehow, like the bus.

As soon as we got under way, I happened to look up and could hardly believe my eyes. Standing to attention in the front of the bus was a small plump Turkish lady in a shapeless dark blue uniform and bulging high-heeled shoes, gripping the back of the driver's seat to keep steady on her feet. A blue bowler hat with the badge of the bus company on it had slipped to one side of her head and her hair was in wisps as if she had just come in from a very high wind. The same bus company badge, only larger, was pinned lavishly on her chest. She looked at us unflinchingly. A bus stewardess! I never saw one again. She lurched regularly down the aisle with her litre bottle of lemon cologne and the candies and shouted, '*Çay!*' very smartly every time we pulled up at a tea-house.

It took us thirteen hours to reach Ankara instead of the usual eight, I didn't know why as we seemed to be burning up the road. I was holding a baby called Cengiz on my lap for some of the time, and I wondered if our stewardess' name could be Zenokrate. At one stop a man just back from Germany went to the front of the bus and invited us all for tea. We drove for an hour at high speed through an opaque yellow dust storm, with no road even faintly visible. I helpfully looked out the window a few times but no one seemed interested, much less concerned, being simply too engrossed in the pleasures of travel.

The School

The school in Uzak Köy had been built in 1960 by the village men of stones and mud and straw. It was the last house at the upper edge of the village, standing alone on the flat top of a rise overlooking all the other houses held within the crescent-shaped embrace of the low-lying hills. It was a small square building with two rooms, one the classroom and next to it a room half the size for the teacher to live in, both opening onto a narrow windowless hall where the winter fuel was kept, wood and dung-cakes piled up to the ceiling at one end.

An assortment of benches and desks, also made by the village men out of rough slats of wood, filled the classroom. The desks were so narrow that they barely held the width of a small notebook and the rows were packed so closely together that the desks were constantly rocked and joggled by the backs of the children in front. Every few days, a bench or a desk collapsed, simply folded up, and Kâmuran grimly dragged the sagging pieces outside. He pried out the long crooked nails and with a stone, hammered them straight to use again. The ends of the boards were honeycombed with holes and it became almost a game to try to find two solid areas to nail together.

There were two small easel blackboards, rough wooden boards painted black. A piece of wood with a wad of sheep's wool tied around one end was used as an eraser. Through the weeks the blackboards faded as they became more and more embedded with chalk and dust. Kâmuran would get an egg or two, separate them, keeping the yolks to eat. He scraped soot from the inside of the tin stovepipe and mixed it with the egg whites, and with this repainted the blackboards a shiny deep black. It was one of the things he had been taught during his two-week teachers' training course.

He had fifty-three children to teach, all in one small room, five classes at once, the little ones in front, the larger ones towards the back. When the weather was warm he organized the lessons in such a way that one or two classes could work outside. A group of children walked back and forth in front of the school, back and forth, like little soldiers, holding their books up high and reading out loud at the tops of their voices. Another group sat against the wall in the sun, scratching out their arithmetic problems with sticks in the dust. When it was cold and raining and snowing, he had to work with all five classes banked up around the steaming stove, coughing and restless, the air thick with the smell of damp wool and wet hair.

The students wore short black cotton smocks, with skirts like little dresses, that buttoned up the back, and around their necks round white celluloid collars that always hung askew like miniature clown collars.

Classes began at nine o'clock, but by seven-thirty most of the children were already playing around the school, a sort of hopscotch traced in the dirt, or catch with a cloth bag full of sand. They had no real games and there were no toys for the younger children. I had thrown out an empty aspirin tube, quite far outside the village where the refuse was dumped. A few days later I saw some little boys playing with it, filling it with sand and rolling it along. They had also scavenged a small empty Butagaz can which they kicked around like a football. Once I made little boats out of walnut shells, with square cardboard sails pierced on a sliver of wood and held upright in place with candle wax. I filled a big basin with water and put stones and sand and pebbles around the edge to make land and harbours. The children watched with interest, but when I tried to make a game out of it, showing them how they could blow each side's walnut ship across the basin into the enemy harbour, it all fell flat. It meant nothing to them. They blew energetically once or twice, the shell boats either capsized or remained stuck on some stones, and the children drifted away to more interesting things. They had never seen the sea, never seen a boat, and the concept of a game like this simply did not exist.

Even Tolay, who stood around sometimes watching the children running about in front of the school, had never learned how to play. I threw sticks for him and, if they did not actually hit him on the head, they fell at his feet and he would back away, with a rather prim, squeamish look on his face.

Towards the end of the spring I set up an English

1. Uzak Köy.

2. The schoolhouse where Kâmuran taught and lived.

3. My room.

4. The village cemetery.

5. Circumcision of Teoman's son, Murat.

6. The hearth where Ramazan was born.

7. Meryem holding Ramazan, only twenty minutes old, his umbilical cord still attached.

8. Bahri's wedding. A tractor, hired for the occasion, brought the bride from the next village.

9. The festivities continued for three days. Hacı Mehmet's wife put 5-lira notes in the dancer's mouth.

10. Hacı İsmail, the Muhtar, and İnci, his wife.

11. Kâmuran and his pupils outside the schoolhouse.

12. The spectacular landscapes of Cappadocia.

13. The day I left Uzak Köy.

lesson for some of the older children, the boys who hopefully would be going on to Middle School. They soaked up the new words like sponges.

Although in the village, being able to read and write was of no great usefulness, it was nevertheless acknowledged that some form of non-religious education, at least for the boys, was of value. It gave them an advantage during their military service, and would always be a safeguard against being cheated by the outside world. The Muhtar, the İmam, and the Hoca, the head of the village, the mosque, and the school by their titles, were the three most respected members of the village, regardless of the degree of personal affection felt for them. Disagreement or ill will might be shown in other ways, never through an outward lack of respect or through any confrontation that went beyond the accepted rules of behaviour. They knew they had to live together regardless of their personal feelings. Kâmuran, the Hoca, had intellectually and intuitively adapted to Uzak Köy and had been accepted, yet it had taken him several months to build up this confidence. He now also had their love. The teacher before him had slept with a gun under his pillow, and all the time I was there I never heard his name mentioned by anyone. They had watched Kâmuran, and judged him, not by his qualities as a teacher, but as a village man like themselves. He is kind, they said, he is clean. They made a motion towards their eyes with their hand: his spirit is clean. He was only twenty-two, yet when he entered the room all the men rose to their feet, smiling, and shifted around to offer him the place of honour. His tiny room in the schoolhouse had become an unofficial gathering place for the men. They went there to talk, to play cards, even when he was busy teaching in the next room or trying to work at his table in the midst of their crowded, smoky laughter and talk.

If Kâmuran ever felt impatient or the need to be by himself, or lonely for his own friends and way of life, he never showed it. He was, through the daily routine, sustained by the sincere innate courtesy and generosity of self that the village people showed towards each other. He slept on a camp bed, with no sheets, no pillow. A bookcase of wooden crates was lined with newspapers and held two glasses, a box of sugar, below it a larger box with potatoes, wheat and rice and onions. A towel hung on a nail, an ancient yellowed map of the world and a newspaper picture of Atatürk were pinned on the wall. A dusty rag rug was laid down for guests to sit on. The mice in his room, the cold, the rain dripping through the roof, barely the money for cigarettes, the lack of a winter coat or any clothing that was not second-hand, were not important enough for comment or complaint. He was from a village himself, and although it was much larger and had all the external amenities of a town, his own life had not been very different.

The moments of discouragement that had no recourse to convention or habit or humour came when he was overwhelmed by a sense of futility about his work in the village, not his own work in this particular village, but that of all the teachers in all the villages. How long would it take? Where would the children he taught find the strength and knowledge to continue, consciously or unconsciously, along the unfamiliar path he had tried to lead them? A vision, a breath of the inevitable future, what reality could he himself give to these words?

In 1928 Turkey was 90 per cent illiterate. Atatürk, again with the intention of cutting off his new nation from a past he considered detrimental to modernization and of starting on its own from zero, made the country from one week to the next 100 per cent illiterate by abolishing the old Arabic script and replacing it by a new phonetic Latin alphabet. He scrapped all words of Persian or Arabic source, almost two-thirds of the existing language, and restored corresponding terms of pure Turkic origin. He sent, literally, the entire country back to school. Teams of instructors went into the towns and villages to teach the peasants their new alphabet and new language. Atatürk himself went across the country with donkeys and blackboards and set up classrooms in village squares. He gave lessons in his palace to men and women in formal dress, whom he had summoned to a gala evening and had sat down in front of a blackboard.

But it was difficult to find teachers who were willing or even able to set up schools in the villages. The teachers on hand were urban born and trained, and they could not cope with the desperate poverty of the rural areas, nor were they accepted by the suspicious village population. To deal with this problem, some twenty special boarding schools were established, called Village Institutes. Their object was to take boys from villages themselves, give them ten years of academic and practical training, then send them back to their villages as teachers and messengers of Westernization and the new reforms. The Village Institutes were located outside of the towns, away from any urban influence that might make the boys dissatisfied later with life on a peasant level. But they were being asked to solve an insoluble problem. The young teachers were indoctrinated with modern ideas and values, yet never given a chance to observe at first hand or be part of a society on which these ideas and values were based. They were sent back to their villages with the task of propagating their own incomplete and half-understood conceptions of progress and the modern world. Furthermore, the village people looked on even their own sons with hostility, feeling they had come back tainted by the infidel outside world. The Village Institutes became centres of radical political ideas and the government eventually merged them with the urban teacher training schools.

A moving account of these conflicts is to be found in Mahmut Makal's book, *Bizim Köy, Our Village*, in which he recounts with anger and despair his return as a teacher at the age of seventeen to the village, and the barrier of superstition and ignorance he met on all sides. His book is a heart-rending denunciation of the poverty of mind as well as of material goods of rural life. When it appeared in 1950 it fell like a bombshell into the urban literate Turkish élite, which had remained rather aloof from peasant affairs. Makal was arrested for subversion but later released and returned with honour to his teaching post. His books today are still best-sellers in Turkey.

The young village schoolteacher could be called the unsung hero of Turkey. With a high school diploma and a few weeks of teacher training he is sent into the most remote areas, and required to become an integral part of the village hierarchy. There are some 38,000 villages in Turkey, most of them without electricity, with no roads, no telephones or mail service, no doctors or stores, with only a radio as a vague link to the outside world. The new teacher, with his few possessions in a wicker basket, takes a bus as far as it will go and walks the rest of the way to the village. He may find a derelict schoolhouse that has been used during the summer to store farm tools and to shelter animals, and have to repair the roof, the desks, the windows himself. He must find a place to live where he can, must beg for a blanket and a sleeping mat. He sleeps on the floor, cooks his own meals, washes his own clothes, works into the night by the light of a kerosene lamp hung on a nail, at a rough wooden table unevenly set on the mud floor. He buys pencils and notebooks for the poorest students out of his salary. He teaches as many as sixty children in one room. If he is lucky he leaves the village once a month to collect his salary, get a haircut and buy supplies, and a newspaper. In eastern Anatolia, many villages are snow-bound during the winter months. Yet these are not hardships compared to the solitude of his life. Months go by before any of the men approach him in open friendship or trust. If he takes his work seriously and pushes too far or too fast, he may find himself isolated and regarded with animosity. If he compromises, he risks sinking into the lethargy he is struggling to combat. In either case, there is bitterness and frustration.

Beneath a personal pride in his school you sense a deeply troubled concern about the apathy and prejudice of the village people he must live and work with. On every side the teacher faces the wall of tradition, of the older generation. The masses of Turks obediently took off the fez, yet in the vast rural areas they are still bound to their mosque, fetishism, holy men and superstitions. Women still cover their face. The men believe that women should indeed be veiled, that girls should not go to school, that sports and the radio are an intrigue of the devil. Illness is cured by words from the Koran, written out and folded into a little cloth bag and pinned on a shoulder, or by having the İmam blow on the diseased or ailing parts. The old men sit in rows fingering their beads and say that what their village needs is a new mosque, not a new road. A new mosque, not a new school.

This can be a heart-breaking business for the young teacher. He is often the only one in the village with the terrible awareness of how much must be taught. He sees three or four of his students burning with intelligence and the desire to continue school, and he knows their fathers have not even the money for a bus fare to Ankara: the boys will become shepherds, will work in the fields. He wants to teach elementary hygiene, yet he knows that there is no one at home who will understand these things, and no money even for a toothbrush. He wants to give out the brochures on birth control he was provided with, he knows that many of the women are open to this idea and that the men are against it. If he talks to a woman her husband is always present and she will agree with her husband; to talk to a woman alone is unthinkable. He wants to tell them about the outside world, to try to open their minds to the future, but his voice is drowned out by the click of beads and the İmam's call to prayer.

In theory a teacher is consulted about village affairs and he shares in making decisions. Undoubtedly over a period of time, if he has succeeded in building up a positive relationship with the community, he could have much influence, by his example and his presence, but he is transferred after two or three years to another village, and his successor must begin all over again.

Beyond all this, I sensed a deeper discouragement in Kâmuran, when he faced his own life. Although discouragement is the wrong word, as he was without self-pity. He knew he had come a long way compared to his father, his own brother, to many of his friends, yet he saw clearly the anonymous ineffectual years ahead of him, in larger or smaller villages, a prisoner of time and place and his own confusion. He had been liberated in a drastic way yet not given the stage on which to enact his freedom. It would have to belong to himself alone. He would always be the outsider, continuing to live against the background of his familiar life, as there was no other place for him to go. He had never talked about these things. To whom could he talk? His mother could not read or write, wore baggy bloomers and head scarf and worked in the fields in summer like the Muhtar's wife; the barrier of respect between his father and himself led only to misunderstanding. He saw his own younger brother, who was clever and eager to learn, leave school because he could not study at night in a room crowded with family and relatives, the radio blaring. He had never spoken alone to the young girl he was going to marry. She would raise his children, be the loyal companion his mother had been to his father, caring for any strangers in his home, invisible in the next room.

Again, with my Western outlook, I would say to him, 'Couldn't you go back to school? Get a university degree? That way put yourself more in touch with people who think like you?'

'No, I know myself. It is too late, I cannot change myself or my life now. I think I am lucky. If I was not a village teacher now, I would be a guide for the tourists in the summer. I would sit all winter in a tea-house playing cards. I must wait. My life will be that, like a bridge. I will know what to give to my children.'

Things from America

My father had sent me a plane ticket to New York for Christmas. When I told them I would be going to America for a few weeks nobody was impressed. They had vaguely heard the word, *Amahrika*, it was out there somewhere, perhaps an extension of land on the other side of the Bosporus. If I had said I was going to Germany, which they knew about from the men working there, they would have slapped one hand in the other and said, '*Amaaaan* . . . that's far, far . . .'

Asiye Nedihe the night before I left put henna on my hands. It was meant as a blessing, to ward off the evil eye, to bring happiness. She had been mixing the black paste in a little dish and made me sit on the floor in front of her. Very carefully she smeared the henna over the palms of my hands and around the ends of my fingers. Then she bent my hands into muddy fists and tucked my thumbs inside. Elif was standing by with two strips of old cloth and a needle and thread. They bound the cloth tightly over my fists and she sewed the edges closed around my wrists.

'Wait till morning,' Asiye Nedihe said wheezing with pleasure, 'it will be beautiful.'

I was helpless without my hands, and they put me to bed, wound my clock. Elif said sternly, 'Don't touch your hands.' I woke up a while later realizing I had forgotten to pull out the little alarm button. The henna had dried and my fingers felt as though they were encased in hard plaster. I got the cloth off one hand with my teeth and worked my fingers loose from the caked henna, small clumps of it going over the floor and into the bed. I set the alarm and went back to sleep. I was jolted awake towards dawn, however, by a vicious slap on my undone hand from Elif, muttering under her breath. But the dye had thoroughly taken, and in the morning Asiye Nedihe with approving nods and clucks examined the deep orange palms and rust-coloured nails. It *was* beautiful, this gift, and all the time I was away I felt I was holding a warm living secret in the palms of my hands.

In New York I was haunted by things to take back to Uzak Köy: a nutcracker, potato peelers, scouring pads, a Techmatic razor for Hacı İsmail – I had asked him if there was something special he would like from America and he said, 'a package of razor blades' – earrings for Hacı Kadin and İnci, Hacı İsmail's wife, some games and a blow-up globe for the school, sweaters for everyone in my house, a flute for Yusuf. I wanted a good flute so I went to Schirmer's, but the wooden flutes were expensive and the plastic ones cumbersome. A small plastic one cost more than Yusuf earned in a year. The salesman and I had got into a conversation about the village, when suddenly he thought of something and brought out a fine wooden flute that someone had recently returned and that could not by law be resold. He gave it to me with their best compliments.

I had also the hope of raising some money for Uzak Köy, towards building a new schoolhouse and helping four of the poorest and brightest boys to go on to Middle School. We had often talked about these things and everyone agreed that a new school was desperately needed. Hacı İsmail had been told by the Kaymakam, the Sub-Governor, of their district that if the village could provide the sand and the stones and put down a small deposit, the equivalent of $150, the government would take over the rest, prepare a report, send out architects, workers and supplies and a schoolhouse would be built. All this had remained only talk, since there was no conceivable way of raising the money for the deposit. I had kept quiet about my hopes, talking only to Kâmuran, not to risk disappointment.

I had never done this kind of thing before and I was overwhelmed by the spontaneous generosity of people I knew and others I did not know. A friend gave $200, someone else $300, and so on, until there was $1,500. This was a formidable amount of money translated into Turkish lira, and an even more formidable amount on the scale of village values. It brought the schoolhouse, and three years of Middle School for Halil, Remzi, Celil and Mustafa, within reach. I was beside myself with joy.

*

Two days before leaving New York I received a telegram from France saying that my mother had suddenly died. She had not been at peace in her life for several years, and neither I nor anyone else had been able to help her. She had died without pain in her sleep early in the morning, and thinking of her, only of her, I knew I could not have wished it otherwise. As for myself, it was a venturing into a dimension of solitude I never knew existed. I went to France to try to put some external order in my stepfather's life. In a letter to Kâmuran, I explained what had happened and that I would be coming later.

When I got back to Uzak Köy several weeks later, walking from the jeep to my house, many women came up and embraced me silently. I realized they had received my letter. During the first hours of confusion in my room, Asiye Nedihe sat beside me, held my hand, rocking back and forth, with tears in her eyes. Elif sat beside me too and said, '*Annen gitti* ... your mother has gone.' She began to sing, an improvised song with many verses, in a flat nasal voice, about my mother, in another country, not having been sick, suddenly going away.

In the same way Asiye Nedihe one evening pointed at my little tape recorder and said she wanted to sing something. I turned on the machine and she began to croak out in her old lady's voice the long verses of her song, making up the words as she went along. She was sitting on the mud floor, her feet straight out in front of her, swaying from side to side. After a few phrases, her voice broke, and everyone around her became extremely agitated, telling her to stop, please stop, you will make yourself sick, but without looking up she shook her head, drew in a trembling breath and went on. She was singing the story of her two sons, one of whom had killed the other after that quarrel over nothing, over who would bring bread to the field where they were working. The older brother had gone mad, got his gun, shot his brother. The government came and took him away and he was still in prison. His brother was gone, lying under stones at the edge of the village. Döndü was alone, five children without a father. As she sang, she wept, blowing her nose in her skirts. The other women slowly beat their breasts with their fists and moaned from time to time. The children sat in silence, their eyes brimming with tears. When she had come to the end of the story, Asiye Nedihe simply folded up and rolled over on her side. Elif and Meryem lifted the frail bundle and put her into her bedding. I did not know if I had done the right thing to record this, it was such a private moment of grief. However, the next day she wanted to hear herself, and many times after that. She listened intently, moaning over her own words as she heard them, but as if it were an old familiar story being told by someone else. It seemed to give her comfort to hear it, somehow transfigured and given the dignity of legend.

A few evenings after my return there was a large gathering in one of the houses, I forget why. After the meal, one of the Elders cleared his throat and said in many sentences which I did not understand something directed to me. Kâmuran translated, 'All the men here are sorry your mother has gone, and they say may God send rest to her soul.'

They thought it strange that her hands and feet had not been dyed with henna. They were impressed that she had been buried in a wooden box. I wondered what they would have thought of her grave, a number on a chart in a cemetery in the south of France, buried among strangers in a place where she had never really lived. Their own cemetery seemed to me a much more authentic acknowledgement of death, a scattering of shallow graves heaped with a few sharp stones and overgrown by time, with no names, no dates, the stones slowly mingling with the stones of their dead neighbours, their dust blending into the timeless silence of the earth.

I gave out the presents from New York. The sweaters were immediately put on, inside out, because the decoration of the seams is nicer that way. The blow-up globe too was seized on as the children were about to study the world and Kâmuran had been going to use an orange with a pencil stuck through it as a model. Hacı Kadin turned the nutcracker over several times and said thank you with warmth but I suddenly realized she was thinking, 'How strange ... we have perfectly good stones to crack the nuts with', and I never saw them use it. The same thing with the potato peelers, they had perfectly good old knives to scrape them with, and the scouring pads, perfectly good sand outside each house to scrub the pots with. Even Yusuf, when he first saw his flute and before he had learned to use it properly and grown fond of it, had said to Kâmuran in a condescending way that they had really *good* flutes in Ankara, the bamboo kind with a nice design of flowers painted up the sides.

A few mornings later, İnci took off her scarf to

show me how fine the earrings looked. To my horror I saw she had forced the broad flat clip through the hole in each ear and the earrings hung open and dangling nonsensically, with the flesh of each earlobe stretched taut and white around the metal clasp. I had not realized they knew only the kind of earring for pierced ears and she had without question put it on accordingly. Hacı İsmail took his Techmatic razor to the school to have Kâmuran show him how to use it, making him shave with it first while he watched. He chuckled, but I sensed he somehow didn't take it seriously.

A meeting was called about the money, and other meetings after that, with many plans brought up and discussed. They would build the schoolhouse, as well as a new road, a new piping system from the spring, and a *köy odası*, like a village community house. Everything seemed possible.

I had been worried about how this money would be accepted, afraid they might suddenly look at me with different eyes, as an easy source of income, and perhaps something patronizing or artificial would creep into their friendship. I told them that friends in my village in America had sent the money, people like them who worked hard for their living. They only partially understood; they could not really visualize the source of this wealth in any tangible, significant way. It was providential, immense, incredible, and yet it remained simple. There was no embarrassment of gratitude. They knew how to say thank you, with an innate distinction of manners that allowed me to feel that they and I were on the same side, together contemplating the gift given us, and nothing changed.

A few weeks later, they hired the tractor and trailer from the next village. From early morning until sundown they rode down into the river bed to get stones. At the end of five days on the top of the rise behind the school lay a dozen neat rectangular heaps of stones, shoulder-high and seven or eight feet long, flattened smooth on top. Two weeks later they went out again, two kilometres up the river bed, for sand. All the men helped. Hacı İsmail organized the men into groups and every morning a different group roared up to the school in the open trailer, half of the men going on to where they would dig the sand, half staying at the school to shovel it off. So there were the stones and the sand. It seemed too good to be true. Hacı İsmail and Kâmuran, the Muhtar and the Hoca, the head of the village and the village teacher, then went off to see the Kaymakam of their district, to tell him about the preparatory work that had been done and to put down the deposit. Although they had much more money on hand now, they were not going to mention this; in fact, they had planned to say that the village was very poor and ask if they could make an even smaller deposit. The Kaymakam told them he had just received the new official programme for the next five years from Ankara. The construction of any more new schools in their province was cut from the plan. The only solution was to build the school themselves.

Hacı İsmail and Kâmuran took a bus to the capital town of the province, to see the governor in case he had other or different information. He told them the same thing. They went back to the Kaymakam. He was sympathetic and had been trying to think of ways to help. He suggested that, if the village could in some way guarantee a certain small amount of money, he could get a government architect to come for a day or so and draw up a plan that the village men could follow without difficulty. And so they bargained and agreed on this plan.

Although this was a severe modification of their expectations, it was met with resilience, and Hacı İsmail and Kâmuran came back to Uzak Köy in good spirits. At least they had gone from 0 to 1, always the most difficult.

Hacı İsmail had enjoyed himself during the three days they had been gone. Kâmuran had taken him to the *hamam* in Çorak. He had never been to a bath before and he had liked it very much. 'Did you have a man wash you?' I asked Kâmuran.

'No, I washed Hacı İsmail and he washed me,' Kâmuran laughed. 'Then we went to the cinema, a film from Iran, very dramatic. It was the first time he had been to the cinema, too. He is a good man. He enjoyed it like a child. You must not say anything, but he cried in the cinema. He said after, "*Hoca*, I cried!"'

Stories

Sahib was another shepherd in Uzak Köy, but different from the others in that he loved to talk. He was the poet and the story-teller of the village. He was a giant of a man, towering over the others. He carried the new-born lambs in his huge hands and spoke with a gentleness that seemed incongruous with his enormous size.

'A few years ago,' he began one evening in a sing-song voice, 'a few years ago, many years ago, the head man of a province, the Kaymakam, called in the Muhtar of a nearby village. They had received a big printed notice from the Government in Ankara, that explained about the wild boar problem and said that every village must go out and hunt down the boar in their district, and kill them. For every wild boar tail they brought in, the bank would pay them 12 kuruş. The Muhtar listened and agreed, and went out and said to himself, "What can this be, a wild boar?" He walked back to his village and called a meeting and everyone was there and they all talked, trying to think what this animal could be. A very old man sat up and said he thought he knew, remembered when he was a soldier in the first war and he was in a hospital in Bulgaria, someone had shown him a wild boar. But that was in Bulgaria, not in Turkey, and especially not in their region, where he had lived all his life. "You must tell that to the Kaymakam," said the Muhtar. The next day they all walked back to the Kaymakam's office and after many greetings the old man began to explain that he thought he had once seen a wild boar when he was a soldier in a hospital in Bulgaria, but that had been in the first war and since then, even since before then, no one had seen a wild boar in this region. "What?" shouted the Kaymakam, "This order comes from your Government in Ankara, written by men with brains, and you are standing here telling me that you know better than these men in Ankara? Brothers, go back to your village and do what you are told." The Muhtar and the old man and the Elders who had come along, all walked back to the village and had another meeting and still could not think what to do. Soon a rumour drifted in, about a man in the big market in the nearby big town who was selling wild boar tails for 6 kuruş a piece. They set out again and went to the town and found the man in the big market and he was, as the rumour said, selling tails. They bought up enough to fill a small sack, and they carried it back to their village and the next day went to the bank and got the money for the sackful of tails. A few days later they heard about what happened to the man in the big market. The police had come to get him and take him out of his shop, because they had traced all the wild boar tails to his store, and they weren't wild boar tails at all. Suddenly all the dogs in that big town had begun to walk around the streets without their tails and the police had found that the man in the big market had been catching the dogs at night and cutting off their tails and shaving off all the different kinds of fur and greasing them down and drying them in the sun and then selling them by the sackful, until the police came to take him away.'

You are, of course, on the side of the fellow in the big market. His story follows a tradition that is found in one form or another throughout the dearly loved Turkish folk-tales. He is the man of the people, who rises to the occasion, who tries and almost succeeds. Beyond that, what can you do, except try again the next time. He is Karagöz, the anti-hero of the puppet shadow plays, ignorant, illiterate, dressed in rags, fighting a losing battle. He is pitted against the smooth-talking well-educated man of the big city, and even when he is chased off the little stage under a rain of insults and blows, his defeats are only temporary and he bounces back intact and undaunted.

He is Nasruddin Hoca, stately and stout on his little grey donkey, the wise man with the eyes of a child, teacher and dupe, whose stories are full of the humour of nonsense and confusion of logic. Sitting by a stream fishing for cheese, the villagers say with mockery, 'There is no cheese in that stream, old man!' 'Ah!' answers the Hoca, 'but what if there were?' Nasruddin Hoca's thirteenth-century tomb in Akşehir is a gate with a huge intricate lock – and on either side of the gate, nothing at all. We take ourselves too seriously, he taught.

He is also the peasant whose donkey is starving to

death, no longer able to swallow the dry tasteless straw put in his trough every morning, as he dreams of fresh green grass. The old man goes to the big city and when he comes back a few days later his neighbours see him looking cheerful again.

'How can you look cheerful when your donkey is not eating?' they ask him.

'He is eating,' says the old man.

And there indeed is the donkey, briskly chewing on the old dusty straw, with a pair of bright green glasses on the end of his nose. We heard this story over the radio on a programme called *Köy Odası*, Village House, recited in a sing-song peasant voice. Hacı İsmail and all the men laughed and chuckled, the story was on them, yet they knew it was on them so it was really on everyone else, and they fully appreciated the irony under the surface of this story. Ah, those green glasses. You are cold? You are hungry? Where are your green glasses, brother?

In Istanbul there was a man whose exploits had already become part of this oral tradition. The village people did not know the name of the current writers or actors or politicians, yet they all knew the name of Sülün Osman. He had been in and out of jail many times, and no matter what he did you were on his side also. He had the infallible instinct to recognize his victims a mile away and to give them only what they asked for. One of the favourite stories about him was already told as if it happened centuries ago. Osman himself sat down on a little wooden stool at the base of the huge clock tower on the hill overlooking the Galata Bridge in Istanbul, with a few friends hidden or loitering casually nearby. He has a small box on his knees and from time to time one of his friends comes up to him and asks him a question. He turns around and looks up at the stone clock tower and says something to his friend, who thanks him and drops a coin in the box and drifts away. Osman is biding his time. Sooner or later he sees shuffling up the street an old peasant in traditional Anatolian garb, the baggy şalvar trousers and embroidered vest, obviously in the big city for the first time, with his savings sewed into a little cloth bag under his shirt. The old fellow's eye is caught by the strange comings and goings and the coins piling up in the little box. He stands at a distance and watches, and then, overcome by curiosity, he approaches Osman and asks what he is doing.

'Well, uncle,' says Osman, 'you see, this clock tower belongs to me and when anyone wants to know the right time they must ask me and I will tell them, but they must of course, in all honesty, pay me a little fee for this service.'

The old peasant lets this sink in and he stands back again and continues to watch the coins drop into the box. His heart beats faster and faster. After an hour or so he has decided. 'Will you sell your clock tower, brother?'

'Uncle,' answers Osman with a laugh, 'you could never afford it. It is a gold mine, as you can see, why should I want to sell it?'

They talk and talk, and argue and argue, and the old fellow finally pulls out his bag of savings and shakes it in front of Osman, 'Here ... Here ... More than this you cannot ask for, all my savings, all the money I have in the world...'

Osman reluctantly gives in, signs over a piece of paper with the old man's name on it, pockets the money, installs him on the chair with the little box on his knees and vanishes down the street. The old man sits until the sun goes down, and sits again for two more days, at the base of the clock tower, and then he goes off to the police.

Cappadocia

There was a one-week holiday and Kâmuran and I were going again to Ürgüp. We had planned to leave at three o'clock in the morning, walk to Bulutlu to get the six o'clock bus to Çorak and from there a bus to Ankara and then to Ürgüp. Around noon the day before, Halil, one of the students, came rushing in to my room with a note from Kâmuran: 'We go now Kırşehir. Come.' I stuffed my big basket with the bare necessities, a pillow, a book, a towel, soap. Kâmuran was waiting outside, empty-handed.

'Suitcase? Basket?' I asked.

'Suitcase in here,' he said with a laugh, patting his raincoat pocket, which contained a deck of cards and a toothbrush.

By luck a jeep had come to Uzak Köy to deliver a pedal sewing machine to the house of Hacı Mehmet, as part of his daughter's dowry, and the driver was willing to take us all back with him to Kirshehir. This was in the opposite direction from where we were going, but that did not seem a problem. At least it did away with the long cold walk the next morning and there were just as many good buses going from

Kirshehir to Yozgat, then to Ankara, then to Ürgüp.

The jeep bumped along the stony river bed for several kilometres, then climbed to the right onto solid ground, and followed a sketchy rough track. The driver was a fat cheerful man, stuffed into a threadbare overcoat. His car, an old Willys jeep, dented and clattering, was cheerful too, hung with plastic tulips, plastic lace and bright blue glass beads against the evil eye dangling from the mirror. In the middle of a tricky manoeuvre across a stream, he hoisted himself to one side and brought an apple out of his pocket which he handed back to us over his shoulder without a word.

We drove through many villages, all looking the same, the same children, same dogs, packed mud walls, muddy fountain, dust and cold. Yet I knew from our village how each was unique and deeply its own. We drove across a wide flat area at the outskirts of a village. A group of little boys was sitting on the side of the road; we waved to them as we had been doing all along, and a few of them jumped to their feet and waved back. As we passed, a stone hit the back of the jeep. The driver skidded to a stop. Hamid, his assistant, already had the door open and had leapt to the ground before the car had come to a standstill. The boy who had thrown the stone was running across the field and Hamid sped after him. The driver was shouting, 'Run ... run ... run...' They ran and ran and the distance between them slowly closed. The boy tripped and fell and Hamid was on him like a dog, kicking him back into the ground, pitching him from side to side by his shoulders and again and again cuffing his head with wide swings of his arm. From a house at the edge of the village a woman came running towards them. The boy was not moving and Hamid came loping back to the jeep, panting and pleased. Around another turn, a brace of partridge crossing the path scattered across the dusty track. The driver chortled, hunched over the wheel, accelerated and drove through them. He pulled to a stop and he and Hamid jumped out and began running up one of the slopes beating into the stubbled grass. A minute later they were back, Hamid carrying the soft, limp, headless body of a partridge.

We arrived at Kirshehir five hours later – it was only five o'clock but already dark. In honour of the holiday, four huge torches were burning at each corner of the monument to Atatürk in the main square. From a tea-house came the hard deep beat of a drum, uneven, fitful. You could not hear the second, fainter, beat, made by a long supple twig held taut and flat against the underside of the drum and plucked in twanging burring syncopation to the stronger thud.

This town looked like so many other Turkish towns: the beginning of a plan of streets and squares, abandoned a long time ago and left to accumulate an overgrowth of stones, broken pavement, piles of dirt; a few sidewalks with curbs so high you had to jump them. Even the way people walked in the streets seemed random and disorganized, carts, bicycles, donkeys, vendors, going in every direction, men stopping to talk in the middle of the road, children chasing each other around them. There were two hotels near the main square, with big signs in garish colours and modern cement façades. In these non-tourist hotels you pay only for your bed, since the room is shared with anyone who comes along or is already there. Sometimes as many as eight strangers welcome each other as they come through the door. A woman, however, must pay for all the beds in a room, as it is unheard of that another single woman will come along. Once I had to take a room with five beds in it. The owner of the hotel was upset as it meant I had to pay 50 lira. When I came back from supper, he had dragged three of the beds out into the hallway and set them up along the wall. Two of them were already bear-shaped with sleeping forms, and the third had a pair of shoes under it. With a big smile, he held up two fingers and said, '*Maşallah!* what wonders God wills ... only 20 lira!'

Now I had a room with two beds and an actual bathroom. It was a dark cement cell, hard to imagine ever having been new. The faucet stuck out of the wall two feet above the sink and the water splashed forward in a wide arc against the front rim of the basin. You could see the floor through the drain, the water ran directly out onto your feet. One of the men at the desk asked if I wanted a bath. He said he would be right up to clean out the tub. There was no plug, as Muslims should wash only in running water. The bath-water ran out the side of the tub through a small pipe near the floor, and eventually down a hole covered with a wire mesh in the centre of the cement floor.

Early the next morning I went out to have breakfast in a small *lokanta* across the street. I asked for some bread and jam or cheese and coffee. This is not the usual provincial Turkish breakfast and it took some time to assemble. A boy was sent to a grocery store down the street with two little dishes and he came back with a square of white cheese in one and some roseleaf honey in the other. He was sent out again to order coffee from a tea-house two doors away, which another boy brought in a few minutes later, swinging the tiny cup on a round tin tray suspended from a metal tripod with a loop at the top for a handle. You pay him directly and he spends his whole day delivering tea and coffee up and down the street, going back later to collect the empty glasses and cups from shop counters or desks or off the pavement in front of a store. The waiter flourished a big white cloth, and smoothed it out half under my plate, half over my lap, thereby serving both as tablecloth and napkin. Only the bread actually came from the restaurant, yet he laid out all the imported items with as much panache as if he had made them all himself. Everyone else was having soup.

When I got back to the hotel Kâmuran was sitting downstairs looking pleased.

'Have you had breakfast?' I asked.

'Twice,' he said, smelling very much of garlic.

*

I was happy to be going back to Ürgüp, the Valley of the Churches, one of the most haunting landscapes I had ever seen. The eruption tens of thousands of years ago of Erciyaş Daği, one of the two sombre volcanoes rising over the Anatolian highlands, created this fantastic country. The soft volcanic mass spread over Cappadocia, slowly baked and hardened into layers, then split open into rifts, ravines and valleys, washed and consumed over the millenniums by hot springs bursting through the rock and by melting snow rushing down from the mountains. The layers of rock crumbled, the great boulders and ledges crashed into the narrow ravines, leaving sheer banks like fortress walls jutting overhead. In the open plain, wind and water swirled around the harder rocks embedded in the soft volcanic tuff, and left cones and pyramids and spires clustered together in lunar villages of grey stone. A massive tidal wave of soft white limestone flowed imperceptibly over the plain, thickened and died; it is still there, as if halted only momentarily in its journey through time. This spectacular surrealist landscape itself would be enough to nourish the most demanding fantasy, yet somewhere in its past it was given another and deeper dimension. Into the cones, spires, pyramids, the straight steep walls, the soft limestone folds, were carved a multitude of dwellings. The smallest cone holds one room, the large ones several, dug out in storeys with doors and window openings spiralling up to their apex. The soft stone was suited for this type of excavation and only a rudimentary architectural instinct was needed to create a network of dry, airy rooms that were fresh in summer and warm in winter.

With time the rains came through the widening fissures, great chunks broke away, doors and ledges slid down the slopes, floors collapsed, and the Turkish government obliged families to move out of the more dangerous caves and onto open ground. Yet the tradition continues. In most villages built up against the hillsides, at least part of every house is rooted in the actual rock. The walls, inner rooms, steps leading from one to the other, the trough for animal fodder, all are cut directly out of the living stone.

These villages scattered over the hills overlook the vast dead cities deserted by their populations of the past. What is left is some fifty cave churches, with their extraordinary frescoes, and an infinitude of pigeons. The intricate network of abandoned caves in the sheer rock made an ideal habitat for these birds who came here centuries ago. They are not considered a nuisance; on the contrary, their droppings have become the main fertilizer for the dry, white topsoil which the wind shifts relentlessly and the rains wash away year after year. The entrances to the caves have been bricked up to leave only room for the passage of the birds. Some of the entrances are marked by rough strokes of red paint radiating from the edges, like giant eyes with red eyelashes set unblinking in the flat stone walls. Once a year the labyrinthine internal passageways, known only to their owners, are penetrated and the precious fertilizer is gathered up.

The genius of the countryside is one of solitude and silence – of summer insects and swelling fruit, a dog barking, a distant voice calling, muffled by the lustrous heat, remote on the edge of sound. The narrow river bed cutting under the vast cliff agglomeration of the pigeon houses of Üzengi runs through light and shadow. Through the silence reverberates suddenly the ubiquitous cooing of pigeons, echoing softly, suffocatingly, from side to side. If the rock were basalt and the trees pine, it would be a place of nightmare. But the colours are tender and sweet, silver and cream, the pale green of poplar and the richer green of apricot and walnut, the darker green strokes of onions growing sparsely in minute plots of ground sheltered between the smooth white undulating limestone mounds. Grapevines grow at random, lushly, spreading out their tendons like clusters of giant green starfish sprawling in the powdery earth.

The two-storey library in Ürgüp has a modest collection of old volumes and portfolios of prints on the Cappadocian churches and I had often been there during the spring to study them. The director of the library was an efficient, energetic man, quite well known in Turkey. Years before he had begun a circulating library throughout the area. He had a team of seven donkeys and three horses, which he loaded up with books and sent out every two weeks into the neighbouring villages. In 1963 he was given an International Volunteer Award for outstanding service. He later bought a Ford mobile unit. There is a photograph in his office, of the shining new truck stoutly flanked by seven little donkeys with their book boxes.

The early history of Cappadocia belongs to the uncertain history of Anatolia, in turn under the Hittites, the Greeks of Alexander, the Roman legions, and in the later seventh century the Arabs. By this time the Christian communities had already taken root in the cave dwellings of Cappadocia, through the centuries digging deeper into their stone shelters. By the end of the ninth century Byzantium again controlled the area and the Christian centres entered their golden age. No rock was uninhabited; the smallest cave chapel, able to hold only a dozen worshippers, was adorned with the word of God; processions wound through the lonely valleys and you seem to hear even now their song ringing from hill to hill.

The origins of these churches and monasteries are also uncertain. With the triumph of Christianity and the liberation of the church by Constantine in the fourth century, there must have been a tendency in many devotees to seek again the solitude and wilderness of Palestine and Egypt. At this time, Basil, born in Caesarea, now Kayseri, and one of the founders of monasticism, may well have gathered about him a group of men who answered his preaching of withdrawal from the world and who sought with him a place of retreat and rebirth in the ghostly Cappadocian rocks. The final dissolution of the Christian communities came about gradually, and by the turn of the century many of the cave churches had been invaded and desecrated. The Greek population and the Orthodox Church, reduced to rather miserable conditions, kept a small hold in Cappadocia, but with the exchange of Turkish and Greek inhabitants in 1928 this too came to an end.

The Muslim inhabitants of Cappadocia are conscious of living close to something of interest to the outside world, yet they seem unimpressed by the artistic miracle that had taken place in their extraordinary landscape. Some of the more remote, unvisited churches or chapels are used to shelter animals or to store fodder and farm tools. They give no official name to these places, calling them simply Greek Church or after the name of their village, or nothing at all.

One afternoon I found by chance one of these nameless churches, high up in the deserted hills, surrounded by tiny vineyards and small white powdery patches of onions. The dark entrance carved into the face of a rock pyramid was surmounted by a rough-hewn cross and some crude Greek inscriptions. There were no frescoes visible inside, only the broken remains of some columns and the small semicircular apse with its stone altar block. A low dark passage led into another sanctum dug deeper into the rock, which served as a shelter during enemy attack. A faint light came through a small opening stuffed with leaves and cobwebs. I had a strange feeling, standing in this infinitely silent cave, as if there was the mute presence of something beyond the barely visible vaulted ceiling and the soft dusty earth under foot. Suddenly, to my left, loomed out of the dark the massive form of a millstone, standing upright in its stone trough, higher than my head, still ready to be rolled forward to close the narrow passage I had just crawled through, still ready to shut out the invader, as it had done how often, how long ago . . . eight, ten, thirteen centuries ago? How many lives had it saved, how many people had crouched behind it, immobile and shuddering? I felt the tears come to my eyes quite inadvertently – I could hear my own heart beating in the unhonoured heart of this timeless stone refuge.

Medicine and Sickness

A few days after my return to Uzak Köy from Cappadocia, Suna's little granddaughter died. Nebaat had been a fat beautiful baby, and the only child of Cemal, Suna's oldest son. Suna herself was beautiful, still young and full of a laughing, graceful vitality. They were very poor, and their house had no matting on the mud floor and only a few dusty cushions at the end of the room. A thin frayed rope was strung across one corner, with bits of clothing and her husband's wooden staff hanging from it. On a window-ledge was a stack of ashtrays hammered out of pieces of tin cut from a Mobil Oil can, and a scratched tray with four little tea glasses in four painted saucers; in the centre of the room the usual small tin stove. Otherwise the room was bare. Suna's own youngest child was only a year old and she had sat with both babies in her skirts, stroking their faces in wonder at how alike they looked.

She had stopped to talk to Meryem that morning, in great agitation, striking her chest again and again with her fist. She was going to the school to get her son, who was playing cards in Kâmuran's room. She burst into the room full of men without hesitation, a very irregular thing to do, especially in a strange house, and pulled Cemal's sleeve. He passed the cards to the man behind him and followed her out. The game didn't stop. Suna was crying and very pale, and she flung out at whoever might hear, 'Nebaat, *çok hasta* ... very sick, very sick.'

That evening one of the young men came for Dursun, who was sitting chatting with Asiye Nedihe in front of the fire. He got up and they went out. I had recognized the names of Suna, and Sultana, the baby's mother, and the baby's name, Nebaat.

'Something has happened to Nebaat?' I asked Asiye Nedihe.

'*Gitti* ... gone!' she answered.

The men were gathering to sit with the grandfather and the father. Asiye Nedihe got ready to go herself to sit with Suna and the baby's mother.

The next morning I went to their house. About a dozen women and their babies were sitting around the empty room. Suna stood up and embraced me. She held me very close, her face against mine. She was crying and I could only say in English, 'I'm so sorry, Suna, I'm so sorry...' holding her by the shoulders. Sultana got up and also embraced me, very tightly, and began weeping in short, high, piercing cries, ten, fifteen, twenty cries, and I tried to tell her also, 'I'm so sorry, Sultana, so sorry.' We sat down, the other women swaying and moaning and wiping their eyes with their skirts. We talked about Nebaat; she had been sick only a few days. It was something in her chest, she couldn't breathe, a few of the women made panting, choking sounds to show how Nebaat had struggled for breath. I could see it so clearly, the swaddled bundle kept close to the red-hot stove, the air heavy and turbid with smoke and dust; at night when the stove was out and the room icy cold, Nebaat laid deep amongst them in their wool bedding, under the thick covers, smothered and gasping.

It was difficult to sustain an atmosphere of mourning, the intention of these gatherings being precisely to provide distraction and force the mind away from grief. The conversation shifted and a few minutes later the talk was about something quite different. There was laughter, even from Suna and Sultana, coming as spontaneously as tears.

Two other babies had died since I had come to the village. The first one shortly after I got there, so I never knew him. The second was a little girl, just over a year old. Her mother was only sixteen, and it was her first child and was sickly from the day it was born. She carried the half-alive staring creature everywhere, sagging against her shoulder, unable to hold up the weight of its own head. The baby's arms and legs were fleshless, her tiny cotton dress hung emptily and oversized around the scrawny body. The pulse in her throat, throbbing like the giant heartbeat of a naked baby bird, pumped with a strength greater than her own and her head bobbed faintly in echo to each beat. She never cried, never smiled, never ate. I saw her in many houses, each time a different woman holding her in her lap, vainly trying to feed her, bread softened in water, soup of mashed wheat, but the baby's eyes seemed to say, 'Don't try.'

Then one day the mother was walking with her arms empty and I asked where her baby was. '*Gitti* . . . gone!' they said. There was hardly any talk about this baby's death, as if somehow no one had felt it had really been alive.

Many of the babies and children had some form of skin ailment. It was usually on the head, and mothers pulled off the babies' little cotton bonnets to show their scalps, dry and crusty, with patches of hair gone. Older children had sores at their mouths and noses and around their ears. Sometimes a father or mother came to the school to ask for medicine, but without conviction. Skin eruptions were treated with mud. And the İmam was consulted. Religion and magic seemed closely allied, charms and fetishes part of daily life. The İmam, for a fee, blew on the infected area, moistened the skin and with a pen wrote a few letters of Arabic script on the diseased spot. Or he wrote a few words from the Koran on a piece of paper and this was folded into a little cloth bag and pinned on the child's shoulder or cap. One of the poorest women came to the school once to ask Kâmuran if she could borrow some money, 10 lira. Her thirteen-year-old son was in Ankara and he was ill. She needed the money for the İmam who had promised to write the healing words on a paper for her, which she could send to her son. Kâmuran himself did not have money to loan, and he was angry to think of it being spent in this way. He offered to write the same words for her and charge her nothing. She thanked him civilly but did not come back. Maybe she knew that he would be using the

Latin alphabet which does not have the power of the holy Arabic script.

There were no doctors in the region. The nearest place with any medical facilities was Çorak, forty kilometres away. This is not perhaps a great distance on a map, but to get there meant leaving Uzak Köy at three o'clock in the morning, walking eight kilometres on foot or with donkeys as far as Bulutlu, from there taking the six o'clock bus to Çorak, thirty-four kilometres, a two-and-a-half-hour ride. In winter with the track deep in mud neither man nor donkey nor jeep could move in or out of Uzak Köy.

The previous winter, Salih's wife fell ill, with a high fever and much pain. When after two weeks she was only worse, he put her on a donkey and they started out for Bulutlu. It began to snow and soon the track disappeared, the donkeys slipping and blundering in the blinding wind. Salih's wife suddenly lost consciousness and slid off the saddle into the snow. He managed to get her inert body propped up in front of him on his donkey and they arrived many hours later in the pitch dark, nearly frozen, speechless with exhaustion, and were lifted down by the Muhtar's son in Bulutlu. His wife lay motionless and burning for two days, then they put her on the metal bench at the back of the bus and took her to the hospital in Çorak. She was there two weeks, got better and was brought home again. This time the sun was bright and the snow firm. She lay another week on a mat near the fire and then got up. From the confused description, the great clots of blood she lost and the high fever, I guessed she had

had a miscarriage and possible puerperal sepsis, but they themselves had not enquired about it at the hospital.

When Hacı İsmail had been in the army twenty years ago he had learned how to give injections. He did this now whenever anyone asked him. The complaints were not cryptic: rheumatism, colds, pains in the sides, middle, bowels and chest. Hacı İsmail kept his equipment in a scuffed brown leather briefcase hanging on a nail in the main room of his house. Inside the briefcase was a dented tin box with some needles, a pair of giant tweezers, several huge glass syringes wrapped in a handkerchief, and a supply of penicillin and sulfa from a French pharmaceutical company, given him regularly by the Turkish Red Crescent. The penicillin went into the arm, and the sulfa into the buttocks, it was up to you if you wanted just the one, or both.

During the coldest weeks in February, Kâmuran had slowly been coming down with a bad case of influenza. He continued teaching, you could hear his deeper cough amid the persistent cacophony of the children's coughing around him. The tin stove was roaring in the centre of the schoolroom, the air full of dust. Before the stove was lit in the morning and afternoon, the tiny room was glacial, with little drifts of snow blowing in through a broken window pane and encrusted on the mud ledge. Hacı İsmail on his own had decided to give Kâmuran an injection. With some leeks and a slab of fresh bread wrapped in a towel under one arm, and the brown briefcase under the other, he pushed open the schoolroom door and gestured roughly for Kâmuran to go into his room next door. Some students followed them in and put a few chunks of dung into the stove. Hacı İsmail sat down on the dusty mat under the window, opened the flap of the briefcase, spread out the syringe, ampoules, and tin box on the floor around him. He fished in the bottom of the bag for the tweezers and, carefully wiping his hands on his trousers, with the tweezers lifted out a needle from the tin box and neatly laid it on the mat by his stockinged feet. He fitted everything together and threw the empty vials into the corner. Kâmuran bared his arm and Hacı İsmail strapped his handkerchief tightly around the upper muscle. He jabbed around under the skin for the slippery vein, pulled the needle out and went at it again from the other side. When he had finished he packed up his equipment, gruffly called out, '*Çay!* Tea!' to the two boys standing raptly by the door, patted Kâmuran on the knee and beckoned to me.

'Let's play cards.'

We had a warm cozy afternoon, cracking walnuts into piles by our feet, drinking hot tea, with Hacı İsmail in high spirits and winning, and Kâmuran pale and light-headed. The blurred sound of the children moving and coughing came through the wall from the schoolroom next door. The next day Kâmuran said that all the card-playing men had ended up in his room, playing until past midnight. He had finally climbed over them onto his camp bed and had fallen asleep, fully dressed, feeling like a baby, he said, lulled by the voices and rocked in his bed by the backs of the men leaning up against it, jolting it lightly each time they bent forward to pick up a card from the floor.

As with so many aspects of their daily life, they seemed to accept illness and pain without question, and to tolerate pain without complaint. There was no sense of urgency or alarm, or that a sick person might merit special care or attention. The routine of life went on. If a man were sick he simply rolled up, fully clothed, even wearing an overcoat and cap, in his bed, on the bare floor or in a corner and turned his face to the wall. People came and went around him, the children laughing and crying, the door banging. İnci, Hacı İsmail's wife, sat through long days of fever on the floor near the stove, swaying and nodding, her mouth dry and her eyes dazed, with many layers of clothes on and a heavy scarf around her face.

Asiye Nedihe crept into a corner like an animal, and lay in the straw on the floor, pulling a man's ragged overcoat over her head. If the sun was warm she lay down directly in the dirt in front of the house, a mound of old clothes and old bones under the overcoat, a bare dust-caked foot sticking out at one end.

'What's the matter with Asiye Nedihe?' I would ask.

'*Hasta!* Sick!'

One afternoon Emirel, the Muhtar's son, brought a strange boy to my room. He was from a village four kilometres away and, with his older brother, was a shepherd. His brother that morning had fallen into a fire pit and had badly burned his foot and leg. He had come to see if there was any medicine to give him. We went to the school. Kâmuran winced as the boy told him more fully what had happened to his brother. In the school First Aid box were two tubes of aspirin, a small bottle of iodine and two half-empty bottles of hydrogen peroxide. He gave one of them to the boy and made him repeat over and over how they must try to pull off the charred clothing, clean the foot and leg with the medicine, put oil on the burns and try to take his brother to Çorak. Kâmuran said to me in English, 'They must take him to the doctor now, now ... but they will never understand this.' The boy nodded impassively, and put the bottle in his pocket. My heart sank as I watched them walk away, sauntering down the slope arm in arm, the shepherd boy with his wooden stick clamped jauntily under one elbow and his head up close to Emirel's in long conversation.

Toothaches seemed to be the most common cause of misery. In Uzak Köy their teeth were rather bad: all the old people were empty-mouthed or had one or two brown prongs still crookedly surviving. The younger men and women had many teeth missing and the rest were discoloured and broken. One of the first things Hacı İsmail had asked me was if the teeth I had were my own. 'Nice,' he said.

Kâmuran claimed the water had some corrosive property, which ate into the enamel and left a design of yellow ridges across the front teeth. Most of the people had never seen a toothbrush, and the few who knew what it was for had never owned one. Whenever I brushed my teeth, squatting in the corner of my room, spitting at the little hole in the floor, anyone who happened to be there would watch wordlessly, tilting their heads to the side, with bemused and pleased expressions on their faces, but not really curious as to the purpose of it all.

One of the prettiest girls in the village was named Hatice. She was quiet and thoughtful and had a lovely way of gravely bending her face towards whomever she was listening to or whatever she was looking at, as if to encompass what was before her more fully and privately. She was only fourteen, and her face had pure lines of beauty far beyond her age. Yet her mouth too was already beginning to decompose and, when she smiled or spoke, it was a shock to see the yellow ridges and unhealthy gums.

A few of the people had been to a dentist at one time, but generally they pulled out their own teeth, with a pair of pliers or a thick string or wire, after sitting for days in silent agony holding their swollen jaw in their hands. Their neighbours held them down and it was always a very bloody affair. The Muhtar's sister-in-law had gone to a dentist in Ankara many years earlier. He had hammered a silver casing in one single strip in and out and around her six front teeth. Through the years the teeth, one by one, had been coming lose at the roots. When she spoke or ate, the entire metal front of her mouth shunted back and forth in a terrible way. One day the last root gave way and the whole thing simply fell out of her mouth, which was a relief for everyone.

On a trip back from Ankara. I went to one of the small general stores in Çorak down the street from the hotel to buy some socks. An old farm truck had just stopped outside in the alley behind the shop. Two men had lifted down a heavy figure and were trying to get it through the door and seated on a wooden chair in the back. The man was in agony, dragging his right leg, useless and cumbersome, behind him, as if he were pulling along the weight of some angry animal which had clamped its jaws onto his foot. The man stumbled against the chair and sat down heavily, sideways, twisted around, hugging the back with his arms.

The shopkeeper nervously opened and closed some boxes and frowned over at the group of men in the back. Shortly another man came through the door – a grey, stocky, poorly dressed, unsmiling man. He went directly to the man in the chair, squatted down in front of him, pulled the foot towards him and roughly tore off the shoe and the sock. The ankle was swollen to a hideous size and the flesh was smooth, taut and yellow. He took the heel in the palm of one hand and with the other bent the thick, stiffened arch forward. The man jerked and twitched into a rigid contortion, heaved his shoulders over the back of the chair, dropping his head forward as if he were going to retch. The man on the floor gripped the foot more strongly, and wrenched it forward again, more violently. The man in the chair grunted, snorted, his voice strangled in his throat. The shopkeeper and I were staring at each other.

'Why don't they take him to the hospital, for God's sake?'

'There is no doctor today, it is Sunday.'

'But there's a doctor somewhere, he must be somewhere...'

'Perhaps, but today is Sunday, and the doctor of the

hospital, he does not know about these things. Only things about the inside of the body.'

'And this man here, does *he* know about these things?'

'Yes, he is the man here who knows about these things.'

Some children came in, the shopkeeper got down a box of thread. The man in the chair was crying, his voice soft like a woman's, pleading, rising and sinking in rhythm with the grim manipulations of the man squatting in front of him. They had not said a word to each other.

Water

The only water in Uzak Köy came from a spring in the centre of the village: two pipes jutted out from a low cement retaining wall, and a thick steady flow of water splashed into a cement trough and from there flowed into another longer trough at right angles to it. The cattle and sheep were herded every morning and evening to this longer trough. Brown mud oozed around the spring. Some flat stones had been set in the mud but they were no real help. When you tried to step from one to the other, a heavy bucket of water in each hand, you slid more often than not into the mud and lost a lot of water trying to keep your balance.

I suffered in my American brain, and asked Kâmuran why they could not fill in that muddy area with stones and sand, in the same way they had built up a stretch of the mud road at the edge of the village. Obligingly, that same afternoon, he took his fifty-three students down to the spring, organizing them into little work gangs, the smaller children carrying sand in their school aprons, the larger ones scavenging for rocks and stones. Within an hour they had packed a dry gravelled surface all around the spring and troughs. Everyone was pleased, especially the women, and it lasted ten days before the mud began to ooze up again. To create a proper foundation, they would have had to repeat this process several times, but, as in so many of their undertakings, they seemed to follow a pattern of enthusiastic and immediate execution of an idea, appreciation of results while they lasted, then a passive looking-on as things sank back to their original state. A dozen men sat most of the day on their heels against a wall of a house near the spring, who could in one afternoon have done this work, not to speak of the school children, yet the thought did not occur to them. They were not lazy or afraid of work. In the summer they worked in their fields until they were numb with fatigue and their hands were cracked and bleeding. They sat back now against the frozen earth, caught in the inertia of the lifeless winter months, with no initiative beyond the daily imperatives.

It was true that the spring was more in the women's domain and touched the men only indirectly, yet even Kâmuran, who was the only person in the village with a genuine awareness of all that needed to be done, fell, for different reasons, into the same lethargy and, when prodded, said only, 'Yes, I know. Later perhaps.' He knew that when he left the village in the early summer, whatever work had been started would be abandoned and forgotten. In spite of myself I could feel this same discouragement and how easy it was to take refuge in the usual rationalizations leading to 'Later perhaps'. I looked at the neat piles of stones and sand that the men had worked so hard to assemble for the new schoolhouse and that now flanked the school unattended and I closed my mind to the awful invading thought, 'This, too?'

Even with water being something you had to measure out, the women were constantly washing clothes and hanging them to dry on the dead spiky bushes that surrounded a few of the houses. Somehow, any apparent dirt seemed 'clean', coming as it did from dust and dried mud, and in summer being burned clean by the intensity of the sun. Even with the scant supply of water in the houses, they managed to wash, especially the men who followed the ritual ablutions before prayer, washing their hands, face and feet in a corner of the room several times a day.

The women cooked on the floor in the semi-darkness of a small centre room, where the fire burned in a dug-out hollow in the far wall. They cleaned the tin and enamel dishes and soot-black pots with handfuls of sand out in front of their houses, and rinsed them in cold water from a large pot. In the room where the folded bedding was piled and the sacks of grain stored there were high shelves, like shallow bookcases, and the women set their few dishes along them as if they were on display. Cotton pouches nailed flat on the wall held the six or eight spoons of the household in individual little pockets. Even the poorest houses were swept and kept in order. There were refinements, too. In some houses, when you left, you would find the mud-crusted rubber shoes you had kicked off in a pile outside the sitting-room neatly standing side by side, washed and dried inside and out.

Many families shared communal latrines, small, dark, mud hutches with no doors. A big hole was dug at one end and some stones or a piece of log worn smooth embedded in the ground in front of it. In some of these latrines you were out of sight in the corner, in others you were in full view. In my own house, when I asked Asiye Nedihe where their latrine was that first day, she showed me the narrow open lean-to behind Yusuf's house. She handed me a broom, and I groaned to myself, but this was for keeping the dogs away until they got to know me. Yusuf's *tuvalet* was one of those in full view and I walked around it self-consciously those first days and could not bring myself to go in. Instead I went further along the hill to the little mud school latrine. It was divided in half, one side for the boys and one for the girls, very small and very low so you had to stoop down to step inside and remain stooped once in. It was built on a steep part of the slope and the ground in front of it had been further dug away so the floor projected over the incline and the holes were open to the air. It was angled so that the girls' side was also in full view, however it faced out onto an empty landscape.

Frequently Tolay would stroll along there with me and in a companionable way stand at the entrance, wagging his tail and peering in, or actually squeeze half-way in and, eye to eye, give great affectionate nuzzles into my neck almost knocking me over. In winter the icy wind whistled and howled up through the hole in the ground, and everything became quite a feat, even trying to keep the paper I used from being blown right back up in my face. Sometimes, especially with Tolay's amiable wagging shape filling the entrance, I would lean my head against the wall and begin to laugh, it all seemed so wildly improbable.

On these occasions Muslims always use water to clean themselves, as paper is forbidden. Paper might have written on it a holy word or phrase. In every *tuvalet* in Turkey there is some form of water. In the modern Turkish hotels and restaurants paper is supplied as well. An attendant sits at a table outside the lavatory with the roll of toilet paper and a bottle of cologne on a table in front of him. When you come out he neatly tears off two or three sheets of toilet paper for you to dry your hands on, while he sprinkles you with cologne.

Most of the toilets are what is called Eastern, a flat white porcelain basin in the floor with two huge flat corrugated footprints on either side of the drain. In places where the European or sit-down toilets have been installed the seats are scuffed and scarred from the shoes of those who are unaware that a different approach was necessary. Even people who do know the difference will continue in the Turkish fashion, repulsed by the sit-down procedure, finding it unhygienic and unclean.

There was never the slightest prudishness about these things. In fact it seemed such a matter of indifference that my own self-consciousness quickly disappeared. I realized this one morning in Bulutlu, waiting for a jeep going to Çorak. I had asked one of the men in a low voice where the latrine was and he had waved up the hill to one behind the gendarme quarters. But wait, wait, he said urgently. He went into the little teahouse and came back with a rusty can full of water, which he handed to me with an efficient nod. I walked past the rows of men sitting out in the sun, many of them waving and smiling good-morning, someone called out, '*Nerede?* Where are you going?' and I shouted back, '*Tuvalet!*' without a thought.

In Uzak Köy there was no easy way to take a real bath, although one could always wash by heating a bucket of water and trying to keep the room warm, but it seemed like a squandering of water and valuable fuel. Every five or six weeks, Elif did have some form of bath regardless of the temperature. Whistling with cold through chattering teeth, she crouched in the corner of my room, scooping the warm water over her head with a small tin cup and rubbing a hard cake of grey soap over her scalp. Her hair reached down to her waist, spreading over her broad back and shoulders like a wet black shawl. She washed with a cotton rag and dried herself with a larger piece of cotton.

Later, on the floor, Asiye Nedihe, with Elif between her knees, combed out the still-wet hair and began rebraiding it, taking long thin tails and deftly interlacing the strands with her crooked old fingers. She passed each half-completed braid to the front over Elif's shoulder and Elif continued braiding it down to the end, flipping it back over her shoulder when it was finished. Asiye Nedihe wove a piece of string a few inches from the bottom through the twenty or more symmetrical braids and tied the string so the braids were held in place in a flat curtain across Elif's back. She never undid her hair in between times, yet she always looked trim, with the top of her hair smoothed down with her fingers every morning and the tidy swathe of fine black braids swinging across her back below her white head-scarf. At the hotel in Çorak there was no place to have a bath either. On each floor there was a dark cement shower stall, but no hot water, and the faucets had long ago locked with rust and disuse. Washing for Muslims must be done in running water, so it is not surprising to find bathtubs mainly in the newer hotels where tourists are likely to stop.

Everyone, however, goes to the *hamam*, the public baths, and they are everywhere, except in the villages. The larger towns have separate *hamams* for men and women; in the smaller towns with just one *hamam*, there are special times during the day for men and women, or they use it on alternate days. The women take wooden or cardboard suitcases or metal buckets with a complete change of clothes and they stay for hours, sitting in the steam and chatting with their friends in the dry room outside, waiting to catch their breath again. They bring oranges to eat or buy water from the attendant, for the heat and dampness is enervating and, they say, hard on the heart.

Some of the older *hamams* have low domed roofs, sparsely studded with thick round inlays of glass, the only source of light inside. In the dressing-room you hang your clothes on a hook with everyone else's, strip down to your drawers and put on a pair of wooden clogs. You follow an unlit stone corridor that seems to turn and tunnel further and further underground. The floor is wet, and the rough walls clammy with moisture, and water drips from the low arched ceiling. As you go deeper the heat increases, it gets darker; your lungs distend in an effort to breathe; the walls and floor are running with heat and unseen water. You go through a small wooden door into a dim vaulted room, hotter still, sound and movement muffled by the ubiquitous presence of water; you already feel you are drowning in hot wet air; you feel light-headed, almost drunk. Naked, half-naked, forms slide through the obscurity; others are slumped immobile against the walls. A pale ponderous figure sits cross-legged in a corner with a child cradled between her huge knees, looking like a primitive goddess of fertility giving birth through the secret folds of her thighs. All blends into a stifling illusion, a netherworld of sleep-walkers, an underwater sanctum roamed by the spectral wives of titans, dimly perceived through the ebbing distance of your own surrender to the heat and water.

Hot water flows continuously into stone basins around the room, splashing over onto the floor. For a small fee an attendant washes you. She is half-naked too, streaming with water. You sit, strengthless, on a stone ledge and she takes your hands and feet in turn, holding them like some lifeless objects, and begins to rub with a coarse cloth in long strokes up and down the length of your arms and legs. Small grey pellets roll and crumble from your skin. She pushes you down flat and flips you over like a fish on the slippery stone ledge, and massages your front and back. In some *hamams* they use, instead of soap, a soft clay, perfumed with orange or rosewater. They wash your hair with this too, pouring buckets of hot water over your head as you gasp for air. The attendant rubs the flat of her hand over your face and gouges her thumbs into your ears and with hanks of your own dripping hair wipes the clay from around your eyes. You creep blindly back along the corridor, into the bright, dry dressing-room, and sink back on the broad ledge, swathed in dry towels, giddy and disembodied. Slowly you begin to see the other women around you, pulling on their clothes, laughing and talking, eating oranges, packing their things. Your own skin is tender and smooth and vulnerable. You are loath to put on rough clothes again and to go such a long way back out into the cold. Much later you understand the mystery of these places, the regression to childhood, to the womb.

In Çorak there was only one *hamam*, open from six to one for men, from one to seven for women, and again for men from seven to midnight. It was not an old-style *hamam*. The square cement building could have been anything, a cinema or a warehouse. The women at the door were open and friendly, inside there was an atmosphere of an informal private club. Beside the large communal bath, there were small individual bathrooms with an adjoining dressing-room, freezing cold, a few nails in the wall to hang your clothes on, and a wooden bench covered with oilcloth to collapse on later. In the small closet-like bathrooms a cement basin projected out of the wall, low down on the wall, under a faucet. You scooped the water out of the basin with an old tin can. One afternoon I was sitting here, the hot water splashing in luxury over the edge of the basin, waiting for the room to properly heat up, when the door opened without a knock and three young women crowded one by one through the entrance and stood in a semicircle around me. One of them pointed to the water and said she wanted a drink, the others giggling with embarrassment. Wanting a drink was a poor excuse, but the girl who had spoken went and cupped her hand under the faucet. I felt a fool, stark naked, talking to these girls fully dressed in shoes and coats and scarves. Yet they were so sweet and their curiosity so real that we had a long broken conversation, about where I was from and how many children they had. The attendant came along and made them leave finally, not because of any possible impropriety, but because they were letting in too much cold air.

In the Muslim culture one of the requisites of cleanliness and of aesthetics is the removal of hair from the body. The men as well as the women, by whatever means is customary, pull out, cut off or shave all hair from under the arms and the pubic regions. It does not take long to make the switch in your own mind and to come to regard anything else as unsightly and repellent, almost obscene in a way.

Love

Bahri's wedding took place in the middle of March. It was a prominent event as Bahri's father, Mehmet, was one of the two or three better-off men of the village. His oldest son had been working in Germany for many years and sent money regularly to his father. Some of this money Mehmet used to go on the pilgrimage to Mecca, and he was therefore a Hacı. When he was young he had been very poor and had stolen sheep, but he was now, as Hacı Mehmet, a pious self-righteous soul. Most of the older men no matter how unruly their earlier years, when they reached a certain age suddenly became afraid of dying. To calm their fear and make up for lost time, they devoted their days to prayer. The bridge into Paradise is narrow, as narrow as a hair, and each prayer and act of obedience to Islam makes each step a little safer. Because of the money from his son in Germany, Hacı Mehmet had a big transistor radio and a modern kerosene lamp and he kept his grain in sacks made of carpeting. In the main room shiny velveteen tapestries hung on two walls, a scene of a turbanned sheik on a white horse with a fat veiled woman slung on the saddle in front of him, galloping away from a harem enclosure under a starry sky; the other was of the sacred *Kaaba*, the square stone building in the courtyard of the Great Mosque in Mecca, containing the Black Stone said to have been given by Gabriel to Abraham, and the most sacred spot to which all Muslims turn in prayer. Hacı Mehmet's grandchildren wore over-sized plaid windbreakers with zippers, sent from Germany. His wife was enormously fat. She had had a stomach operation a few years earlier. One day she pulled her bloomers down over her huge flabby abdomen to show me the scar. It ran in a fine line straight down the middle of her belly, as if someone just a moment before had run the point of a knife lightly through a tub of leavened dough. The navel was gone, one pale raisin swallowed into the yeasty mass.

Their seventeen-year-old son Bahri was marrying a girl from a nearby village. They had been engaged for two years yet he had seen her only once during that time, when he had gone with his family to her village. Bahri had sat aloof in the family group, and the closest he had seen the girl was when, with her eyes lowered, she had passed the tray of tea glasses around the room. She had never accompanied her family when they came to call on Hacı Mehmet.

Marriages are arranged in most villages by the parents. They base their choice not on an individual girl or boy as much as on the family as a whole, its background, standing and reputation. There follows a long procedure of observation, discussion, bargaining and simulated reluctance before both families finally come to terms. One of the crucial questions in deliberating a marriage is the bride-price, the sum of money paid forth by the father of the boy to the father of the girl. This is in no way regarded as a commercial transaction, but rather a formalization of negotiations between two families in the marriage contract. The amount varies from region to region and in Uzak Köy was set at the staggering sum of from 8,000 to 12,000 lira, £500 to £750. In a poverty-stricken village like Uzak Köy this seemed ruinous. A man with many sons had to borrow money, sell his fields and sheep, tie up the rest of his life trying to pay back debts. Yet it was the custom, and a matter of pride, so the money was always found. Debt itself carried no disgrace.

In the remote villages there is still no civil legalization of marriages and it receives only a religious blessing by the local İmam. Bigamy is now against the law, yet in 1963 there were known to be half a million second wives in Turkey. Four men in Uzak Köy had two wives. The last wedding that took place was that of Dursun, marrying a second wife. He was twenty-five and in the eight years of his marriage there was only one child. He married a young girl from another village, from a highly respected family and the second wedding was a festive social occasion. His wife was fifteen, shy and pretty. She was welcomed into Dursun's family with pride, taking up her duties quite naturally alongside the first wife. I often saw the three of them sitting, with Dursun in the middle, laughing and chatting together.

The legal age for marriage is seventeen for a boy and fifteen for a girl, although in the villages not much attention is paid to this law. By marrying at such early ages the young people in a way pass over adolescence and step directly from childhood into adulthood and the social roles they were being prepared for all their young lives. As turbulent as the children are, when they reach puberty they suddenly seem to take on a dignity and gravity far beyond their age. A thirteen-year-old girl going to the spring to get water walks with her eyes lowered, passes a relative or neighbour as if he were a stranger. The boys at thirteen stop running, walk slowly and soberly like the men. I never saw a man run or move quickly. Only after a certain age did a few of the women seem to relapse at times into a playfulness among themselves. I always had the impression of moving among men and women of the world.

It was almost unheard of for a village boy or girl to remain unmarried, even the most backward or unattractive. In Uzak Köy one of the young girls was exceptionally homely, with a long misshapen nose, no chin and strabismus in both eyes. I pondered over her and asked Kâmuran if she too would find a husband. Of course, he said, there are many villages around here and someone, maybe as homely as she, will want her and she will be happy like everyone else. There was also a young boy who when he was a baby had had a disease that left him childlike, with a stutter and nervous twitching. He was a shepherd. He kept mostly to himself although everyone liked him and made him welcome. He was a sweet, good-natured boy and had an endearing way of calling Hacı İsmail '*Muhtarım* ... my Muhtar', and Kâmuran '*Hocam* ... my Teacher'. His family had begun negotiations with a girl's family in a rather distant village, but when her family finally came to Uzak Köy and met Sait they called off the plans and angrily went home. Sait will probably be the only unmarried person in the village.

In my own mind I struggled against the idea of marriage arranged in this fashion. What possible chance did they have, knowing nothing of life or each other, thrown unaware into the quicksand of human relationships while they were still almost children, to be together until they die? But here was a different truth. The men and women of the village were not yet victims of the present-day vicissitudes of the soul, their instinct for happiness was still without guile, they still had confidence in the life they were leading. In their marriages, if at fifteen they do not fully love yet, they grow to love later, with the steadiness and devotion that comes from simply living their life together unquestioningly, knowing without knowing that they must share the burden of survival until the end of their days with this one man or this one woman at their side. Their lives are still guided and held firmly within the scaffolding of tradition with its rules of behaviour rooted in self-respect and respect for others beyond and above individual idiosyncrasy. Their private morality and their public morality are one and the same.

A person can grow old in peace, untouched by the fear of solitude, knowing he will sink deeper with the years into the protective shelter of his family, surrounded by the sum total of his life: his children, grandchildren, great-grandchildren. The days are a man's own property, he is a part of everything that happens around him; he knows who he is, where he is; everyone is here, everything is here.

Kâmuran himself was engaged to be married to his cousin. With his progressive view of life he talked about how they would move away from their families, live alone in their own apartment, travel, have a modern free life. At the edge of his mind he would have liked to believe this, but he knew he would not know how to do it. He had been engaged for two years and he too had never been alone with his cousin, had never spoken to her alone even in her own house, and this in his eyes was as it should be. I dared to ask him if he loved her.

'Now? No...' he answered thoughtfully, 'but I know I *will* love her.'

Through all the months I was in Uzak Köy there was hardly a flicker of curiosity about who I myself was, where I had come from, what I had done before or was thinking of doing next. That I had lived in many places, had worked for a magazine, a newspaper, had taught school meant nothing, except perhaps they could vaguely picture a mud schoolhouse similar to theirs somewhere in the world. What impressed them was that I was an only child, that I had never known my grandparents, that my mother and father lived separately in different countries and that I had no husband and no children. These were awesome facts. I think they felt that the dissolution of my family must have come about through some terrible misfortune, the village of my grandparents ravaged by some great cataclysm, my father uprooted and left without land, without sheep, my mother unable to work and too weak and sickly to have other children. In their experience of life my own life was empty.

Hacı Kadin came one morning to see me. She took my hand and we sat side by side and in hesitant words she tried to explain, that it was a very good thing to have a good husband, that it was beautiful to see your children around you, like little animals at first, then growing, men and women with their own children, but still yours, always yours, from your own blood. To live peacefully in this village was good, it was a good village, the people were good, clean, standing clear in front of themselves. 'We will be planting soon,' she said, 'and everyone working again and the summer is warm and full of fresh fruit and vegetables to eat.' These were the truths of life that she thought I should be told. She heard her own words and for a flashing second a bewilderment crossed her face as if she had come close for the first time to understanding herself the immensity of the meaning of her words. I felt my throat tighten and I wanted to tell her, 'Oh, my dear, it is too late now . . . if I could be born again . . .' She seemed to sense my thoughts and roughly put her arms around me. I felt a great love for her well up.

Hacı Kadin was a venerated woman in the region, everyone knew her and talked of her goodness and devoutness. As many men came to see her as did women. She had been born in Eastern Anatolia when it was still part of the Ottoman Empire. That region after the First World War was designated Independent Armenia but within a few months Atatürk had retaken the area.

Many families of Turkish origin were uprooted and dispatched into western Turkey to settle where they could. Hacı Kadin's father was killed. She was separated from her mother and sisters and sent to a remote village in Middle Anatolia. Barely ten years old, speaking only an Armenian dialect, she found herself suddenly orphaned and terrified in an impoverished family of strangers. Through the next years, although they were kind to her, she thought only of going home. A man from the vicinity took to coming to the village and one day told her family that he wanted to marry her. She did not like him, but he promised to take her back to Armenia if she married him. She agreed. After they were married he took her three kilometres over the hills to his village, Uzak Köy, where she has lived ever since. He was much older than she and had had five wives before her, all of whom had died. Hacı Kadin had seven children in seven years and then her husband died, too. She had never grown to love him deeply, she said, but she was very happy with her children.

It was difficult to disentangle family trees. There was much intermarriage among families and the lines of kinship were blurred, even the terminology of relationships varied from region to region. Hacı Kadin would pat the arm of almost every person who came to visit from the nearby villages and say proudly: '*Benim!* ... mine!'

'Your brother?'

'No, no, my grandson!'

'How many grandchildren do you have, Hacı Kadin?'

She raised her coarse hands and made clumsy counting gestures with her fingers.

'Ninety? One hundred? More!'

And I began to understand that she counted all the offspring of her husband's long-ago wives as her own grandchildren, even when they were older than she was.

In the flow of their daily lives husbands and wives came together often during the day, yet at the same time they each had an independent existence. The men, the undisputed pivots and decision-makers of the household, spent much of their time away from home with the other men out of doors or in the Muhtar's guest-room, in male circles which the women would not think of penetrating. The women had their own domain closer to home, cleaning, cooking, their children, helping neighbour women or visiting nearby houses, accepting their position as part of the natural order of life. Husband and wife did not depend primarily on each other for companionship, they did not weigh on each other. They never became small through discourtesy or competition or demands.

There was never any public display of affection between husband and wife, yet they did not conceal their attachment. Whenever İnci, Hacı İsmail's wife, went with a group of women to visit relatives in another village Hacı İsmail became restless and absent-minded and the other men teased him. He spent most of the day at the school playing cards in Kâmuran's room, and looking more and more out of the window. When he finally saw İnci's small figure walking, walking, on the horizon he got up without a word and went out to meet her.

They had been married for twenty-five years, he teased her and told her she was old, yet he called her '*Kız* ... girl'. Sometimes he gave her a push or prodded her with his stockinged foot and she looked at him with a serene inward smile.

Bahri's wedding festivities lasted three days. At six in the morning of the first day, the three ambulant musicians who had been hired began to play in the open area in front of Hacı Mehmet's house, two dour men with a bass drum and a clarinet and a young man who danced. The dancer wore a full woman's skirt of faded cotton down to his ankles, with an absurd little ruffled peplum around the waist. He twirled, dipped, stomped across the snow-crusted ground, chinking tiny brass finger cymbals like castanets. The music would stop abruptly. The dancer froze in his tracks, his hands suspended above his head. He waited, listening. Slowly his fingers began to twitch out a faint rhythm, then louder, louder. A suggestion, a command, for the rest of his body to answer as the drum and clarinet suddenly burst out wildly to join him in a whirlwind of music and dance. He was very good. Hacı İsmail and a few of the older men danced too, slowly, in a long dark row, their arms over each other's shoulders, in the familiar Balkan fashion, the men at the end flicking a handkerchief in measure to their dipping and stepping. The women sat watching in bright clusters on the roofs of the houses overlooking the scene, while the other men sat on their heels against the wall below them. Hacı Mehmet's son had come from Germany for the wedding, with a lot of money and German cigarettes. Hacı Mehmet's fat wife waddled out pretentiously every few minutes to put a 5-lira note in the dancer's mouth as he whirled by, or place it on the ground where he twisted into a back-stand to pick it up between his teeth.

For two days the men had been coming from all the surrounding villages, coming in small groups over the hills. As they approached Uzak Köy they fired their guns into the air to announce their arrival. Hacı İsmail and the Elders and any other men, led by the drummer and the clarinet player, walked in a group out of the village to meet them. The drum thudding and the clarinet bleating wildly, the music echoed over the empty hills, as they went out to meet their guests and escort them back into the village, like kings going out to meet kings.

Every evening there were parties, the men in one room, the women in another. The women sat packed together on the floor in an incredible confusion of laughter and chatter, eating walnuts, apples, sticky pink and white candies. A young woman perched on the window ledge drumming out a rhythm on the sides of an empty oil can sang in a high nasal voice. In a small space in the middle of the room two girls danced, snapping their fingers and moving in short steps tightly around each other. The room was a carpet of laps and knees and arms weighed down with babies and children. As a child fell asleep his mother heaved him up out of the mass and he was passed along like a small bag of grain from hand to hand across the room and finally lifted, still asleep, onto the back of someone near the door who carried him home to his bed.

Hacı İsmail had a large gathering at his house the second evening, with the drummer now playing the *saz* and the clarinet player singing. The young man danced, his skirts flaring out into the faces of the men cramped together on the floor. Kâmuran and most of the men got very drunk on raki that second night, and the next morning the school was closed.

Many of the men had revolvers left over from their army days and they flourished these whenever possible. At weddings there was always much shooting, to celebrate. The morning after this particular evening at Hacı İsmail's, they counted thirteen bullet holes in the mud wall at the end of the room. One of the gun-slingers was a young man whose left hand was wizened into a three-fingered claw, someone at an earlier wedding having accidently shot away half of his wrist and hand in festive exuberance.

Early on the last day we went to Hacı Mehmet's house to wait for the bride. It was bitterly cold, the frozen mud tufted with snow. Many people were already there. The musicians were playing; Bahri was inside, in a room with the men. A tractor, hired for the occasion, was bringing the bride and her family from their village, with one stop at the cemetery at the edge of Uzak Köy where the İmam was waiting to pronounce the ritual prayer. Suddenly there were gunshots and shouting. The tractor with an open trailer hitched behind came roaring and bumping into the village and lurched to a standstill in front of Hacı Mehmet's house. Someone was standing in the back of the trailer waving a Turkish flag, Bahri's older sister was holding up a large mirror –

the largest mirror possible is borrowed, to make more luminous the luminous day of a wedding – shots were going off in all directions, children running in circles, all the dogs barking. The bride was sitting motionless on the floor of the trailer, her head and entire body wrapped and concealed in a huge purple cloth. Bahri's older brother leapt into the trailer and picked up the swathed figure, swung it over his shoulder and struggled up the steps through the crowd into a side room full of women. He set the figure on its feet against the wall and the women closed in around it, singing in high short voices. The figure stood dumbly against the wall, the women pressing around it, examining the gold coins around its neck that showed through the folds of the purple covering.

That evening she saw her husband for the second time, alone and speaking to him for the first time. Sometime during the night a sheet of their bedding was tossed into the next room, the stains examined and there was the final jubilation among the parents. Bahri then went into another room to sleep, the customary gesture towards a new wife that first night. The next morning a few of his friends went around the village collecting gifts in his honour, cigarettes, an apple, an egg, whatever you had.

I asked Asiye Nedihe and some of the other women if Bahri's wife was pretty. They all said eagerly, oh yes, she was very pretty, very pretty. I went to see her a few days later, wondering how she was surviving, plunged as she had been into a household she did not know in a village she had never been to, cut off from one day to the next from her own home and family and being only fourteen years old. She was sitting on the floor with the other women cheerfully at work kneading bread. She had a thick-set figure, small eyes close together squinting out of a round red face, yellowed teeth and a bottom-heavy jaw. It was hard to think of her as pretty in any way. What they had meant was that she was kind and good-natured, was strong and healthy and good with children, knew how to make bread and to cook, and would be a loyal and loving wife.

A bride is called *gelin*, which can be translated figuratively if not literally as 'the one who comes'. In theory, she is at the beck and call of the older, more established women of the household, is expected to do the menial work, wait on the mother-in-law, and only speak when she is spoken to. This holds true for the young daughters of the family as well and a new *gelin* is fortunate if there are still unmarried girls at home to share her lot with. If she does not get along with her mother-in-law her life can be hell. The stability of her marriage, at least in the early years, depends almost more on the relationship with her mother-in-law than with her husband. Her position becomes easier when the desired son is born. Although she will love a daughter as much, she knows daughters soon marry and leave home, whereas a son is a permanent possession. A woman with a son will never be left homeless or in need; a son will bring a *gelin* into the house to work and serve her in her own old age and she will be able to watch her son's children growing up around her in security.

The Beginning of Spring

Through the last weeks of March a change had been building up in the air. Even though there were still cold days, wind and snow even, the earth was slowly letting go. Minute yellow and pink crocuses had broken through the crusty bark of the ground, fragile wisps of moist colour miraculously breaking through the jagged clots of earth. The austere stiff branches of the almond trees suddenly thawed into pink and white blossoms. Women sat in clusters outside, against the walls of their houses, protected from the wind, in the sun. The evenings were longer. The air was soft at night, full of deep sweet smells, and the stars seemed to hang closer and glow more splendidly. The men were beginning to prowl through their gardens and walk in groups early in the morning out to their fields, and day by day more women and children went with them to begin to work. I got presents of eggs, still warm. I would find bowls of milk and yoghurt on my bed, and small damp fistfuls of tiny orange wildflowers left by the children. The children were exultant, as they began to remember the spring before. 'Wait until the tomatoes come, they are red red red

... and the cucumbers and the grapes and everything and everything ... We eat and we eat and everything is good...'

The first lambs were born. And every day more, until each family had a wobbly bleating commotion of baby lambs nudging the wooden doors of their pens, waiting for their mothers to come back from grazing.

Often I went up to one of the higher places overlooking the broad river bed below and the spreading hills far on the other side, to watch the flocks coming home in the evening. They came over the crest of the farthest hill, almost out of sight. All you could discern was a faint stirring in the texture of the earth, an almost imperceptible movement forward, as if the surface of the hill itself had come loose and was beginning to slide in slow-motion down the slope into the hollow. Then the landscape lay empty and fixed again, until, soon, along the top of the nearer hill appeared the broad rim of the advancing flocks. It spread slowly over the crest and poured thickly down the hillside, flowing forward as an entity, carried along by some invisible inner momentum, with only a vague ebbing and flowing ripple across the doughy wool carpet of its back. When it appeared again, closer, it had broken up into hundreds of individual sheep, their heads bobbing in rhythm with their plodding steps, and I could see Bekir or Yusuf among them, and Tolay and some other dogs walking along at the edge. They swarmed down into the river bed and began to move more quickly and to bleat, thinning into a narrow file as they funnelled two or three at a time into the path that led up past the mosque and into the centre of the village.

Now in spring, the shepherds usually took another man with them or some of the older boys, to carry the lambs that were dropped during the day up in the hills. You could see the men suddenly gathered around the shaggy heaving form, bending and stooping, and a few minutes later placing a tiny snow-white creature in the arms of one of the children. Whoever brought back a lamb was given a few eggs or a bowl of milk in recompense.

There was a shaggy empty nest on the far corner of the roof of the mosque, and the people had begun to watch it. Every year a pair of storks comes to nest there. They usually had three eggs, but can care for only two and the third egg is found smashed on the ground near the mosque wall. They stay six months, raise their young and fly off again. They have been coming for many years, and the village people say it is always the same pair, as many other storks fly over the empty nest without stopping, on the way to their own nests in villages further north.

One morning some children ran by on their way to school, chanting, '*Leylekler geldi, leylekler geldi* ... the storks have come...' Only one stork, though, the wife, they said. She was standing motionless in the nest, her head raised. A few moments later she skimmed out over the village, flying low over the roofs. Then she went back to the nest. Then another flight out in the opposite direction. All morning she came and went, returning to stand immobile, gazing out over the village. At noon I looked again, and she was sitting in the nest, her wings folded flat around her. Somewhere in her instinctive world was she feeling, 'I am home'?

Two days later a second stork was standing on the rim of the nest by her side.

Leaving

One morning in early June a jeep arrived, with a gendarme and a man from the governor's office, asking to see me. There was some question about continued permission to live in Uzak Köy, and they had come to take me to Ankara. I was given barely the time to put on another skirt and change my shoes. Hacı İsmail was away in another village. Kâmuran tried to find out what was wrong, but the government clerk himself knew nothing. We drove as far as Çorak in the jeep, and there transferred to an official black limousine with a red light on the top, which had been waiting for us. I knew there was still ample time to renew my tourist visa. I knew the local government office was fully aware of my presence in the village; I had been to see the Kaymakam especially for that and he had been more than welcoming. There had been no trouble anywhere as far as I knew. I was becoming more and more frightened.

We arrived in Ankara in the early evening. It was dark and raining. The driver did not know which ministry we were to go to. We drove around endlessly, stopping at last in front of a huge government building, with only a few offices still lighted. We went from floor to floor. In one room sat a young man reading a newspaper. He languidly opened the letter the gendarme had concerning me.

'Hm,' he said, 'not this office. Anyway, it says you must leave the country tomorrow. Why? Turkish law,' and he shrugged and went back to his newspaper.

I tried to control the panic. We went out into the rain again and drove to another ministry. I was put to wait in an ante-room and finally taken into a large elegant office. Three men, elderly, well-dressed, were sitting at a table. They offered me cigarettes and chocolates. I was helpless, still half-dressed in village clothes, carrying my basket, my mind in turmoil. They were kind. One of the men knew a little English. There was a law. Foreigners were not allowed to live in what was demographically termed a 'hamlet' without official permission from the government in Ankara. With no nearby medical services, no constabulary, no roads, no communication, it was a responsibility they did not want without good reason. They were understanding; it was nobody's fault; a law cannot be known by everyone. I was given three days to pack up my things and say goodbye. I could apply for official permission tomorrow if I wanted, although it would take months to pass through the various offices. While I waited I could live anywhere I chose, in Ankara, Çorak, even in Bulutlu, which was termed a 'village'. But not in a hamlet, not in Uzak Köy. Three days.

Three days. The next morning in another office I begged for more time, to allow the women to finish the bead work I had tried to start them on, to have a few more weeks of English for the boys, to see the storks hatch their young, to try to find out what was going to happen to the school, to take Asiye Nedihe on a picnic, and to think of how to say goodbye. I was weeping, the man I was talking to suddenly had tears in his own eyes. He had understood, he was from a village himself. They gave me twenty days.

I got back to Uzak Köy the next afternoon, utterly despairing. I walked from Bulutlu alone, over the desolate hills now warm and faint with green, towards home, understanding fully for the first time that it was now time to say goodbye. It was inevitable, I knew it would have come sooner or later, but not now, not tomorrow.

Asiye Nedihe and Elif came immediately to hear what had happened. Hacı Kadin appeared suddenly. She said, 'You must not worry, everything will be all right. Hacı İsmail is coming now.' We sat in silence waiting for him. Time passed. His mother was becoming nervous and I said, trying to laugh, 'It's all right, he is playing cards perhaps, he is busy, tomorrow he will come.'

Then there were voices outside, the door pushed open, Hacı İsmail came in followed by the four Elders of the village. They came in gravely, ready to meet with me officially. In the midst of my sadness I could not help but feel calmed. He had taken charge, he had done what should be done, and I felt ashamed for having doubted him. The men said they would go back to Ankara with me, *they* were the Turkish people and could have whom they wanted as a guest in their village.

They would explain this to the government and everything would be all right. But I knew they could do nothing, and I did not want them to become lost in the endless dead-end corridors of the Ankara ministries.

The last days are a blur in my mind. The children said, 'Don't go now, we will be eating good things soon, life will be easy again.'

Hacı İsmail wanted to give me a sheep to take back to my father.

'Hacı İsmail, I can't take it. It's a long way. It will die.'

'We will put it in a box, with grass and water.'

They could visualize it as far as Ankara, in its box on top of a bus. Could it be so very different the rest of the way to America? Hacı İsmail gave me finally, for my father, a pair of men's socks in a heavy plastic envelope, that İnci unlocked from their wooden chest of possessions.

İnci came towards the end to tell me they had had an idea, a way for me to stay with them. 'You will marry Hacı İsmail,' she said. 'You will live with us. I will teach you how to make bread. I will teach you how to pray. We will be sisters. Otherwise, maybe you will not come back. Hacı İsmail is a good man. It is very simple.' I was shattered.

I remembered something I had once read that often came into my mind: 'Ah, the truth-tellers of the world, they will not be silent, and they break our hearts.'

Asiye Nedihe again put henna on my hands. Halil, one of the sweet young boys of the village, came into my room late one of the last nights. He stood in the dark next to my bed where I was reading by the light of the kerosene lamp. He said softly, 'Carla, I am crying.' It was one of the things we had acted out in our English lessons, walking, laughing, talking, crying, the sun and moon, bread, water, sheep, goats, brothers and sisters, love and death and silence and song.

Then my suitcase was fitted into a saddlebag, a big stone was lifted into the other side to balance it, and it was put on the back of a donkey. Several men walked with me as far as Bulutlu.

I finished some things in Ankara. My plane was due to leave early on Monday. That Sunday morning I was having breakfast in the little hotel lobby in Ulus, wondering where I would find the courage to sit with myself, knowing how long this day would be. The front door of the hotel swung open, Hacı İsmail and Kâmuran and four other men walked in. They had come all the way from Uzak Köy, to sit with me, as they sat with their neighbours during their moments of grief. We went to the zoo. To the Atatürk Mausoleum. We stopped for ice-cream, for tea. We played cards in the corner of the hotel lobby until very late. The day was being got through. Then we shook hands. Hacı İsmail said, 'Do not be sad now. You will come back. We are waiting for you.'

I had prepared myself not to hear from them. I knew they wrote letters to their sons in Germany, with the addresses crudely printed out phonetically, but to me in New York? Three weeks later an airmail letter came from Hacı İsmail, dictated to someone in Ankara who had a typewriter. A week later a letter came from his brother in Germany whom I had never met. Through the months other letters came. Everyone was fine, nothing had changed. Everyone was there. Let us know what day you are coming back. Again they had taken charge, and I was ashamed to have doubted them.

Kâmuran wrote that Tolay had got himself into very bad trouble. He had stolen two chickens from Hacı Mehmet and killed them trying to eat them. Hacı Mehmet went to Bulutlu the next day and angrily got the gendarme. The gendarme took Yusuf, silent as always, and Tolay, friendly, back with him to Bulutlu. Yusuf was told to pay a fine which he did not have, and Tolay was put in jail for two days.

Then another letter came from Kâmuran many months later. A bitter letter, with nothing in it, like the others, to try to make me laugh. He had been transferred to another village, near the northern coast. He had gone back to Uzak Köy for a visit on his way to his new school. In Çorak, in the market, he had met two of the older men from Uzak Köy.

His letter continued, 'I say to them, Where are you going? What are you doing here? They answer, We are buying wood and cement for the new mosque. I say to them, But the school, the new school? Then I understand a terrible thing,' the letter ends, 'The mosque is coming first, the school is coming later, maybe never. It is always like this, it is our fault for not understanding.'

Oh, poor Kâmuran, poor Muhtar, poor village. Should we have known? Who misjudged? Was this inevitable after all? But it could not be given up so easily.

With the help of a Turkish friend, I wrote Hacı İsmail a series of letters, one after the other, and told Kâmuran to do the same. I wrote Hacı İsmail that I knew he must be busy building the school, that Allah was watching him build the school. I did not mention the mosque. I wrote that he was doing a good and right thing building this school for the children of the village, and that it was Allah's will for this to happen. I felt very sorry for him, reading these letters. He must already have realized consciously or unconsciously that he had not had the strength to resist the piety of the older men and the İmam. Would he in turn now hear the other voice of these letters calling to the other loyalties I knew were equally strong in him?

A long time passed and I knew nothing. Then a letter came from Kâmuran. He had just returned to Ürgüp for the summer. On the way he had again gone back to visit Uzak Köy.

He wrote: 'I walked the road you know. I come over the hill and look down at our village, and do you know what I see? I see one new cement schoolhouse, and behind it another small new cement house, for the teacher, and two small new *tuvalets* in cement, one for the boys and one for the girls. I sit down on that hill, I smoke a cigarette, I look and look, and my heart is like a bird.'